SEVEN
TOMORROWS

SEVEN TOMORROWS

Toward a Voluntary History

Paul Hawken, James Ogilvy, Peter Schwartz

BANTAM BOOKS
TORONTO · NEW YORK · LONDON · SYDNEY

A YOLLA BOLLY PRESS BOOK

This book was produced in association with the publisher
at the Yolla Bolly Press, Covelo, California. Editorial and
design staff: James Robertson, Carolyn Robertson, Dan
Hibshman, Barbara Youngblood, Diana Fairbanks, Joyca
Cunnan.

SEVEN TOMORROWS
A Bantam Book/February 1982
All rights reserved.

Copyright © 1982 Paul Hawken, James Ogilvy, Peter Schwartz
Cover photograph by Stephen J. Krasemann / Courtesy of Bruce
Coleman, Inc.

Library of Congress Cataloging in Publication Data

Hawken, Paul.
  Seven tomorrows.

  "A Yolla Bolly Press book."
  Bibliography: p.
  1. Forecasting. I. Ogilvy, James A. II. Schwartz,
Peter. III. Title.
H61.4.H38   303.4   81-17547
ISBN 0-553-01367-X (pbk.)   AACRS

Published simultaneously in the United States and Canada

Bantam Books are published by Bantam Books, Inc.
Its trademark, consisting of the words "Bantam Books"
and the portrayal of a bantam, is registered in the U.S.
Patent and Trademark Office and in other countries.
Marca Registrada. Bantam Books, Inc.
666 Fifth Avenue, New York, New York 10103

Printed in the United States of America
0 9 8 7 6 5 4 3 2 1

Acknowledgments

THIS BOOK IS THE WORK and responsibility of its authors, but it began as an effort to make accessible to a wider audience the collective work of the futures research group at Stanford Research Institute—now SRI International. The ideas and their form have evolved, but their roots are the work of what began as the Educational Policy Research Center (EPRC), which became the Center for the Study of Social Policy, and is now the Strategic Environment Center (SEC). During its fourteen years, Willis Harman and Arnold Mitchell have played an especially central role in the evolution of the ideas and approach of the group. Many others have made major contributions: O.W. Markley, Duane Elgin, David MacMichael, Thomas C. Thomas, Marie Spengler, Thomas Mandel, Peter Teige, Norman MacEachron, Richard Carlson, Russell Rhyme, Charles Hanks, David Curry, Donald Michael, Paul Shay, James Smith, Hewitt Crane.

SRI draws its support from research contracts, grants, and consulting. A number of companies and individuals have been especially supportive over the years: C.F. Kettering Foundation, Royal Dutch/Shell Group of Companies, the Environmental Protection Agency, Congressional Research Service, Cincinnati Milacron, the U.S. Office of Education, Pierre Wack, Napier Collyns, Ted Newland, Joop DeVries, Diane Boss, Tony Finizza, Fred Talcott, Dennis Little, Walter Hahn.

This book also has its roots in a small research organization, Pacific House, created by David Miller and Peter Shoup and supported heavily by the Weyerhaeuser Corporation.

A number of people helped in the process of creating our manuscript, especially Margaret Wakelee, Ene Riisna, Wayne

ACKNOWLEDGMENTS

Van Dyck, Pam Shaw, Juanita O'Connell, Oso Bartlett, and
Elizabeth McConnell. The quality of the ideas and the form of
their expression were greatly aided by the insights of James
Robertson, Carolyn Robertson, and Daniel Hibshman of the
Yolla Bolly Press, Tobi Sanders of Bantam Books, and F. Joseph
Spieler, our literary agent.

Anna Hawken, Heather Ogilvy, and Funtz Schwartz provided
the humor, detachment, and goodwill that nourished the col-
laboration. Their patience and understanding became in the end
the rarest and most precious contribution of all.

Contents

List of Tables

SEVEN
TOMORROWS

PART ONE
AN UNSETTLED
FUTURE

Chapter I

A Stance Toward the Future

THE FUTURE IS UNSETTLED, yet we need a future we can believe in. Fewer Americans than ever before believe the future will improve their lives. Following years of faith in automatic progress, many Americans have abandoned hope for growth and prosperity. No longer taken for granted by the bulk of the population, the American Dream, like a fading faith, has few apologists. But it is not dead.

The hope for abundance, power, prestige, and success was no more than a dream for most Americans of the Depression Era. In the years following World War II, however, many people's dreams were fulfilled. As it was translated into programs, plans, and expectations, what had been a dream became the Official Future. Its newest version is more cautious. The new optimism purports to be more realistic — a slightly chastened version of the American Dream that nonetheless includes prosperity for all hard-working Americans. The Official Future is embedded in our legislation, corporate planning, and political platforms. It promises greater economic growth and a future more prosperous than the present. But the Official Future may be built on images of yesterday's success rather than today's realities.

We, the authors of this book, do not believe in the orthodoxy of the Official Future. Nor do we accept the simple alternative of pessimism. Prospects of doom paralyze action just as certainly as naive hopes render action unnecessary. A society deprived of all hope suffers a kind of morbidity. Me-firsters scramble for the life-boats while others, having lost the ability to laugh, look on in silence.

We need a future we can affirm, a future that is neither so hopeful as to be unrealistic, nor so grim as to invite despair. Optimism and pessimism are not arguments. They are opposite forms of the same surrender to simplicity. Relieved of the burden of complex options with complicated consequences, both optimists and pessimists carry on without caring about the consequences of their actions. Convinced of a single course for the juggernaut of history, whether malignant or benign, both optimists and pessimists allow themselves irresponsible actions because they believe that individual actions have no significant consequences.

Our book is about the possibilities that exist in the future. We propose seven plausible scenarios for the eighties and nineties. The scenarios are neither predictive nor prescriptive, but suggest that the problems and options that we will encounter require a more rigorous and intelligent stance toward our fate than mere pleas for more goods and less uncertainty.

The book is based on our belief that human choices can make a difference. We present a range of alternatives because the act of choice requires precisely articulated alternatives from which to choose. Furthermore, the nature of the future demands that we respect the genuine diversity of its possibilities. Human choices make a difference because human history is partially the product of choices among alternative possibilities.

What distinguishes us as human is not some invariant and predictable essence that determines a single fate. Humanity is not an inevitable feature of the species *Homo sapiens*. Though its raw material is natural, its biology subject to lawlike necessities, humanity is nevertheless humanmade. It is the artifice of centuries of human history, a collective construct, a great creation engaged in by billions across millennia. This act of collective creativity allows human beings to change some of the rules of the human condition in a way that nature does not allow her wholly instinctive creatures. Human freedom consists in the capacity to invent and to choose a better way to live.

This capacity for inventing a future different from the past has drawn the attention of very different schools of twentieth-century thought. Existentialist philosopher Martin Heidegger calls it *temporalizing*. Marxist humanists speak of *praxis*. Anglo-American philosophers talk about *intentional action*. All reflect a common awareness of the importance of projecting alternative goals, then choosing a preferred path. This capacity for projecting alternative futures, then choosing among them, is as close as anything to being the essence of humanity. All else is instinctive or mechanical, at best the habitual behavior of the animal *Homo sapiens*.

Our aim, then, is to project alternative futures so that responsible and intelligent choice is possible. We are not interested in utopian speculation. Recent studies of the future have been based on increasingly sophisticated tools of research and analysis that have removed future studies from the realm of mere conjecture. Yet the field of future studies is far from the dubious ideal of precise prediction. Scientific inquiry will succeed no better than crystal gazing at seeing a *precisely* predetermined future, for the simple reason that the future is not precisely predetermined. Nor is the future so indeterminate that we are free to invent whatever future we think would be nice. Between the poles of a fully determinate future and a void to be filled by utopian longings, a range of real possibilities beckons both our imaginations and our wills, for the future we will eventually inhabit is largely, though not completely, a matter of the choices we all make in the present.

As obvious as some of these remarks may sound, they seemed called for nonetheless because the best-known works of future studies each focus on one future as most probable. *The Next Two Hundred Years* by Herman Kahn et al., *The Coming of Post-Industrial Society* by Daniel Bell, *The Promise of the Coming*

Dark Age by L. S. Stavrianos, *An Inquiry into the Human Prospect* by Robert Heilbroner, *The Age of Discontinuity* by Peter Drucker, *Mankind at the Turning Point* by Mihajlo Mesarovic and Eduard Pestel, *The End of the Dream* by Phillip Wylie, *The Genesis Strategy* by Steven Schneider, *The Third Wave* by Alvin Toffler, and *Muddling Toward Frugality* by Warren Johnson — each focuses on one particular future. They base policy recommendations on predictions of some events as being more than merely possible. Whether their predictions are bright with a technocratic sheen, as Herman Kahn's have been, or darkly foreboding, as are Robert Heilbroner's, the mere fact of their determinateness has tended to de-emphasize the role of human choice in setting the course of the future. The temptation to describe a singular future arises from the sheer complexity of the world we inhabit. Economists, social analysts, and statisticians have developed abstract and simplified means for viewing the flow of human events. Once these abstracted quanta have been gathered over a significant period of time, few can resist an attempt to discern and interpret patterns that may reveal a predictable, singular future.

A second temptation among futurists is a preference for world-shaking events with high visibility over the commonplace world of day-to-day choices. The wonders of technology and the horrors of ecological catastrophe make for more exciting copy than the subtleties of incremental change. Dramatic events allow more objective certainty than slight changes among subjective perceptions. Yet an underlying premise of this book is our belief that perceptions guide actions as much if not more than facts. The size of our oil reserves is finally a matter of measurement, not opinion. But whatever figure finally emerges as the expert consensus, some will see *enough* while others will perceive a *crisis*. Perceptions often differ even where the relevant facts are demonstrably the same. After the crash in 1929, all of the physical pieces needed for productive capacity remained in place — the factories, the raw materials, the workers. Civilized life is an elaborate tissue of promises, contracts, and agreements based in large part on perceptions. Change the perceptions, whether or not the facts have changed, and the fabric of agreements begins to tear.

Because perceptions are slow to change, social change is a halting thing — two steps forward, one back. Because we attend to the lumbering momentum of perceptions, the tone of this book will be more moderate than either the Hosannahs of the more hopeful futurists or the alarms of the prophets of doom. In order to investigate both the lighter and darker paths to the future without succumbing to the inevitability of either, we will consider several narratives covering the next two decades. Each possible future is cast as a scenario looking back at the same period from the year 2000. Among the many methods for probing the future — from elaborate computer models to simple extrapolations of history — we chose the scenario method because it allows for the inclusion of realism and imagination, comprehensiveness and uncertainty, and, most of all, because the scenario method permits a genuine plurality of options.

The concept of the scenario is derived from the movies. A scenario in film is an outline of the succession of scenes and describes the unfolding of a story. It is more than a synopsis of a plot in that it has more detail, but it is certainly less than the full script. A scenario in future studies functions similarly. It is more than a simple outline of possibilities in that there is a coherent story to be told. But it is less than a future history in that it possesses neither the detail nor the certainty of history.

We believe that each of our seven scenarios represents a real possibility, and that each is distinct from the others. Each is a work of imagination with some novelistic touches added to color what might otherwise be drab trend projections. Drab or not, the data that have fed those projections are the results of more than a decade's research performed at SRI International (formerly Stanford Research Institute). We are eager to make the fruits of this research public because we believe that both its methods and results are important for the future. Its publication is essential to our primary purpose: to increase awareness of the potential crises that face humankind and to highlight the role of human choices in determining the future.

Since the very complexity of world affairs threatens to confuse people into a fixed pessimism, the projection of clear alternatives can free people from the rigid lock of a predeterminism that becomes its own prophecy. Institutions exist by common agreement. Schools, governments, and businesses proceed on the basis of our common desire that they should persist. When people believe that a bank no longer deserves their trust, a run on the bank causes its collapse and confirms their worst fears. Likewise, if we begin this decade with an unspoken agreement that the future will fail us, we initiate a run on the future that begins with the lifeboat ethic and ends with the accelerated extraction of material resources and the rapid depreciation of our social contract.

If we see the future positively, or at least with a modicum of faith, we can and will put aside short-term wants and considerations in favor of long-term benefit. How we see the future has everything to do with how we live in the present. This book is not an exercise in speculation born of curiosity, but an attempt to present the potential future consequences implied by our present choices.

The coming decades are likely to be a watershed, a time that will change much that we hold familiar. While the Hydra-headed problems of reduced energy, rising hunger, increasingly erratic weather, and constant global conflict augur poorly for our collective fate, we do not see that fate as inevitable or the problems as insoluble. The one resource that is boundless and abundant in all our futures is the human spirit. Of all the variables that one must consider when looking ahead, it is the one that remains positive. Ultimately, the future of our country and our planet does not lie solely in external events, but also with the will of its inhabitants.

This basic premise — that the future depends on human decisions and the values that inform those decisions — will not go unargued. We are well aware that the force of this premise will satisfy neither side in the ongoing debate over the nature of social change and the evolution of political and cultural forms. On the one hand, historical determinists are convinced that underlying material and economic forces carry human society like so many ants on the back of a giant, age-old tortoise, whose ambling course has little or nothing to do with the desires or decisions of its passengers. On the other hand, elitists and conspiracy theorists argue that history turns on the decisions of individuals like Napoleon, Alexander the Great, or Hitler.

We would argue that no one is in control of the current course of history, not the President of the United States, not bankers like David Rockefeller, not "the international communist conspiracy." Nor is our fate totally determined by the inexorable dwindling of our resources or by other material and economic forces. Instead, humanity stands at a unique point: simultaneously our problems are so acute and our communications network so widespread that, for the first time in world history, genuinely collective and democratic decisions are both demanded and possible. In order to choose intelligently, we need a sufficiently widespread consciousness of our condition and of our capacity to alter it through the decisions of enough people. We need a collective intelligence of a kind that may not have characterized the human species in the past; but we see no reason to believe that, given the highly developed nervous system of an advanced communications network, a whole population cannot reach a stage of mature self-consciousness much as an individual does.

Despite the limitedness of knowledge about the inner workings of both nervous systems and social systems, cybernetic information theory suggests the possibility of assuming that intelligence is a feature of any feedback system that manifests a capacity for learning. We needn't specify the *exact* mechanisms of memory and information retrieval, whether in the brain or in a culture. But there are new information flows linking institutions with their stakeholders. In a market economy, the theory says that the marketplace is a perfect expression of people's economic desires and that business is ruled by the market. A similar fantasy holds that government is democratically responsive to the will of the electorate. The experience of economic and political systems out of control, leading to a growing sense of powerlessness, indicates the contemporary failure of such mechanisms. But people are potentially better informed through wider education and increasing access to media. Also business and government are increasingly seeking diverse ways to monitor people's intentions (for example, polling, social forecasting, content analysis, and market surveys). It is hardly a democratic process in any traditional sense. But for now it may be better than either rule by self-serving elites or anarchic paralysis.

Such a distributed network of communications and information storage might permit a process of deliberation, learning, setting of shared goals, and their subsequent accomplishment. Past societies have either neglected planning or left it in the hands of elites. We cannot afford to neglect planning because we have global problems that require coordinated planning for their solution. In a highly diverse nation, however, planning by an elite is both undemocratic and rarely effective. Therefore, it is imperative that the society-at-large achieve a forward-looking intelligence.

Like an adolescent whose nervous system is capable of deliberation and responsible action, modern civilization has the physical wherewithal to come of age. Also like an adolescent, modern civilization has a greater capacity for self-destruction than an eight-year-old. Nuclear capability is the driver's license. We have reason to worry while hostile nations cruise around through the teen-age nighttime of international tension. The risks are real, and we will address them in Part Three, where the threat of nuclear holocaust receives the attention it deserves but cannot receive in the context of a scenario. For now we want to dwell not on the risks of physical-technological maturity but on the opportunities it presents.

It is not our place as authors of this book to invent or announce the mechanisms of choice, much less the most desirable outcome for the act of social deliberation. Our objective is simply to articulate the availability of choices in order to make our power to decide more real. Some would treat the future as a *fait accompli*, as something already determined and therefore predictable. Such futurists are rather like parents who confront their children with ready-made careers and then expect them to be grateful. Our interest lies not in any single outcome but in the process of getting there. Will people wake up to the possibility of self-determination, or will we muddle along merely reacting to what an arbitrary history hands us?

Chapter II

Constructing Scenarios of the Future

F OR CHOICE TO BE POSSIBLE, clear alternatives must be available. Each alternative must be plausible and in some sense desirable, otherwise, the clear superiority of one option will lead the chooser to say, with some correctness, "I had no choice." The seven scenarios that follow represent plausible alternatives for America's next two decades. Not just any batch of scenarios will satisfy the conditions for a Voluntary History. This chapter describes some of the conditions that define the bounds of plausibility.

To create the seven scenarios, we first reviewed relevant variables, including food consumption patterns, desertification, demographics, carbon dioxide production, resource distribution, and others totaling about a hundred. To begin construction of the different futures, we identified five basic "driving trends": energy, climate, food, the economy, and values. Although these five do not incorporate all of the variables in our initial review, we discovered that their dispositions would roughly but usefully approximate the states of the other variables. At the same time we found that these five forces would have the broadest effect on the greatest number of people — short of nuclear war or catastrophe. In limiting the driving trends to five, we could more easily study the possible interactions between them and thereby identify those interactions that most plausibly will occur within the next twenty years. The variety of these interactions has lent each scenario a unique character. For example, Living Within Our Means presents a situation in which adverse climatic changes and chronic energy shortages create high food prices and short supply, leading to substantial changes in personal and social values as well as to real changes in lifestyle.

By using five driving trends with several options for each trend — for instance, benevolent or turbulent climatic conditions — we generated a matrix of all possible combinations of those five basic variables. The resultant combinations included some that were clearly implausible: scarce energy, a bad climate, famine, and a flourishing economy do not mix. Other combinations tended to cluster in bunches so that a variation in food supply or climate, for example, did not seem sufficiently crucial to warrant wholly separate scenarios. By pursuing a process of eliminating implausible scenarios and consolidating those that remained, we reduced the range of abstractions to seven concrete possibilities.

The seven scenarios are intended to be realistic. But what does it mean to be realistic? The simplest answer is that the research behind them ought to consist of demonstrable facts, and indeed the seven scenarios are based on a large body of data, trend analysis, and specific studies conducted at SRI and elsewhere (see Bibliography). But a more subtle answer to the question recognizes the idea that facts are in part a function of the method by which they are determined. Since most research focuses attention on only some fraction of reality, to be realistic requires diversity of both people and methods. We have borrowed from the analyses of philosophers the focus on deeper structures of the human condition. From historians, we sought an understanding of the nature of social change; from contemporary social psychology, the perceptual structure of the contemporary world; and from economists, the boundaries set by physical realities and the choices of the past.

Barring cataclysmic change, some dimensions of the present are likely to persist for a very long time. These conditions are the consequences of our past; they constitute the momentum of history. Since the future begins with this present, every scenario must credibly answer the question, "Can we get there from here?" We therefore present a summation of those conditions from the past that constrain our present and future behavior. These are the preconditions that to some extent set the boundaries for all the scenarios, especially in the near term.

DIVERSE SOCIAL VALUES

In the United States, there is a widening divergence of values and lifestyles. Some of these differences have historical and ethnic roots. Other differences originate in the post-war affluence that has granted, at least for the time being, an array of options unknown to less prosperous societies. Whether we continue to be rich, or contract into regional pockets of depressed economies, or something in between, it is unlikely that we will become a more homogeneous nation. Very likely we will continue the movement toward a highly diversified, heterogenous stew of peoples, values, and goals.

Social trends likely to have the greatest effect are the nascent and surging religious revival, which is presently underway in America, and the thoroughly pervasive "majority movement" of the changing role of women. The first has been referred to as the Third Great Awakening and portends pronounced changes in social and individual values. Just as the First Awakening preceded the American Revolution and the Second led to the Emancipation Proclamation and the Civil War, a Third Awakening could have lasting historical impact now only dimly perceivable. Such an awakening would not necessarily mean a greater tolerance for other values, even other religious values. While the more cosmopolitan areas near the coasts are engaging in spiritual practices both exotic and experimental, the interior portions of America manifest a decidedly conservative thrust in their religious awakening.

The women's movement represents the first social movement in history that identifies itself solely on the basis of gender. Although the early stages of feminism met resistance within the middle and lower classes during the sixties and seventies, we see no reason to believe that a new generation will view past resistance as an obstacle to greater roles and power for women. If the old mold of "woman" has been permanently broken, some fundamental values and structures of society must change, too, especially the roles of men.

A TURBULENT WORLD

The overwhelming post-war dominance of the United States and Russia created a bipolar world with a relative measure of coherence and stability. We are now moving toward a multipolar world in which emerging Third World nations challenge the legitimacy of Western modernization and dominance. Some of the lesser developed countries exert influence beyond their size because they control critical raw materials. Since there remains a worldwide impetus toward economic growth, recent constraints on Third World development contrast with excess consumption in the West in a way that makes conflicts more likely and painful. There may not be a world war like the first two, but the world may find itself at war nevertheless with tumult rampant, nuclear capability spreading, and violence and terrorism increasingly used as a means to resolve differences.

SLOW ENERGY GROWTH

Despite decontrol, presidential programs, legislation, and high prices, virtually no new sources of energy will be available to the United States for the greater part of the eighties — except imported gas and oil. Disruption of existing supplies is likely in the unsettled Middle East, and increased competition for energy might come from the Soviet-bloc nations if they become importers during the coming decades. Apart from the possibility of a major depression causing reduced energy usage, conservation measures will be slow in coming because it takes time to change established building and transportation patterns. Given these several constraints on conservation and supply, it is highly unlikely that energy availability will increase sufficiently to fuel a growing world economy. If, during the eighties, necessary action is taken to conserve and develop new supplies of energy, the nineties could be a period of both energy growth and economic growth.

BURDENSOME DEBT

During the last decade individual, government, and corporate debt has increased at twice the rate of inflation and four times the rate of the increase in the production of capital goods. At the same time we need to borrow more to rebuild our capital infrastructure in order to boost productivity, compete on world markets, and save lagging industries. Between 1960 and 1980, corporate indebtedness rose from $154 billion to about $1 trillion. In 1950, corporate debt amounted to 50 percent of the GNP, by 1976 it was over 80 percent of the GNP. A growing fraction of our efforts was required to service our soaring debt.

The government, of course, is going deeper into debt. Between 1960 and 1980 the national debt more than tripled, reaching $914 billion. The private sector has increased its debt at an even faster clip. In the decades between 1950 and 1980, mortgage debt rose from $55 billion to $1,420 billion and consumer debt went from $22 billion to $380 billion.

As we enter the eighties, the United States as a government, as a business, and as individuals is $5 trillion in debt. As long as the economy was rapidly expanding there was the hope of catching up. But in a slowly growing or failing economy, the mountain of debt may overwhelm us. How we handle this $5 trillion mortgage on the future is one of the major uncertainties for the decades ahead.

AN AGING POPULATION

For the past five years each annual projection of the U.S. population has been lower than the previous one. Lately global trends have also started to decline. In the United States this means proportionately fewer students, fewer workers, and fewer consumers in the future. Since much of the impetus toward

economic growth derives from a growing population and the
need to equip new households, there will necessarily be a
restructuring of the marketplace. Furthermore, as we age, the
graying of America means more people relying on social security
and pension systems that are supported by proportionately fewer
workers. The resulting shift of the tax load onto white and blue
collar workers will cause further reductions in real income.

SLOWING ECONOMIC GROWTH

In order to attain strong economic growth — over 3 percent per
year in real terms — we would require during the coming decades
abundant and relatively inexpensive energy, productive and
well-managed private and public sectors, stable global politics, a
growing work force, a good measure of social consensus, and
massive amounts of credit. Since few of these conditions exist at
the present, real growth of the economy, at least until 1990, is
somewhat unlikely.

A SOCIAL LEGACY OF DISTRUST

Certain national and international antipathies are unlikely to
be easily resolved over the coming decade or two. Most of the
polarities carry with them the full weight of some moral if not
religious rectitude, usually on both sides. Each represents a seed
of future conflict and none seems likely to come to a meaningful
consensus or agreement soon. Some are: United States vs.
U.S.S.R., U.S.S.R. vs. China, China vs. S.E. Asia, Arabs vs.
Israelis, French Canadians vs. Other Canadians, Left vs. Right,
Consumers vs. Oil Companies, Environmentalists vs. Developers,
Blacks vs. Whites, Poor vs. Rich, Hispanics vs. Gringos.

NO END TO CRIME

By the mid-seventies, half of all Americans were afraid to walk
in their own neighborhoods at night. A black male between the
ages of twenty-five and thirty-five is most likely to die by murder.
Fear of violence has become a part of the American way of life.

Every measure of crime is rising rapidly. Since 1967 violent crimes have been rising at a rate of over 7 percent per year, with rape the fastest growing of all. In 1979 over 12 million people were victims of violence. If the growth rate continues, by the year 2000 there will be 40 million victims of violence every year. In 1960 there were 600,000 handguns sold in the U.S. By 1979 that number had increased by 400 percent to 2.4 million. The number of people killed with those guns ran right alongside. In 1960 over 4,000 people were killed with guns. During the late seventies, deaths by gunshot ran around 14,000 per year. The public costs of dealing with crime were accelerated even faster as expenditures on crime grew from $3.5 billion in 1965 to nearly $16.3 billion in 1979. By the early seventies, private businesses were spending a billion dollars a year on security and had raised a 200,000-person army to protect their establishments. No other country among the industrialized nations has a crime rate like ours. Death by violence is three to twenty times as likely to occur in the U.S. as in any other industrialized nation.

The only real question is: How long can it go on this way? We are spending more to protect ourselves, but crime and the fear of it are rising exponentially. Somewhere over the next two decades the pattern will be broken. We cannot reach a point where the curves converge a few years past the year 2000 and nearly everyone in America becomes a victim of violence. But how will the pattern of apparently inexorable growth be broken?

CONTINUING ENVIRONMENTAL DEGRADATION

Environmental conditions of a decade hence are on the whole likely to be worse than today. Mining, burning coal, and producing synthetic fuels may lead to severe and inescapable environmental problems. The tradeoff for those who do not want nuclear plants may be more coal-fired plants. If we encounter deteriorating economic conditions in the future, the likelihood is that we will ease environmental regulations in hopes of aiding industry. It is our opinion that it will require far more than two decades to achieve an ecologically benign society.

NEW TECHNOLOGIES

A primary force for change during the last century has been new technology. There are at present two major new technologies, and nothing is likely to prevent their further development. The first is microcomputers and a new generation of computers for both personal and institutional uses. Right behind electronics may come bio-technology, including genetic engineering, sophisticated prosthetics, and technologies to "improve" human intellectual and physical performance. Other technologies that could have major impact are lasers and particle beams deployed from space as both defensive and offensive weapons. Although exploration of space seems a noble human goal that could unite international groups, it seems more likely that weapons will reach space before human colonies do.

RISING LEVEL OF DISEASE AND RELATED COSTS

The combination of increased stress and environmental pollution could produce a cancer epidemic or a rise in chronic diseases. It is possible that we are burning a long cancer fuse ignited after World War II by the increased use of asbestos, pesticides, and additives, and that the disease bomb will explode as the children born after the war reach middle and post-middle age. In any case, cancer is increasing, and along with it all medical expenses, far in excess of inflation or price indices. As Western allopathic medicine becomes increasingly sophisticated and technologically reliant, it becomes less and less medically admissible or even possible for a doctor to provide anything less than state-of-the-art techniques for fear of malpractice suits and a risk to his or her reputation. Up to now most new medical technologies have meant an exponential rise in expenses for the ill. If the trend continues, medical expenses as a percentage of GNP will soon exceed 10 percent, up from 5.2 percent in 1960.

DETERIORATION OF SOIL

The world is highly dependent on the health and condition of its soils and ecosystems, especially in respect to its ability to produce food. Yet the health of those systems has deteriorated greatly during this century. During the next twenty years, climatic changes coupled with high oil prices may demonstrate that soils have drastically declined in their ability to produce crops without the help of fossil fuels. Unlike the historical past when the planet was sparsely populated and new lands were available, we now live in a densely populated world with decreasing amounts of potentially arable land. If American or world agriculture should falter in its productivity, even for as briefly as a year, all of the world will suffer the shock. No resilience within the food production system can cushion the potential impact.

Table 1
The Post-War Era and the Years 1973-1980

The Post-War Era (1945-1973)	*1973-1980*
falling resource prices, unconstrained supplies	rising resource prices, geophysical and political limits on supplies
growing economy, low inflation, high productivity growth, rising debt	stagnant economy, very high inflation, no productivity growth, credit bubble
high birth rate, more workers, students, consumers	low birth rate, slow growth of workers, students, consumers
unquestioned faith in science and technology	growing doubts and limited respect to science and technology
homogeneous values, common goals	increasing social diversity of values and lifestyles
faith in institutions and progress	cynicism, doubt, and pervasive pessimism
rising crime	rising violent crime, culture of paranoia
benign climate, falling food prices	variable climate, agriculture system overstretched
growing private and public bureaucracy	growing tax rebellion
male social norms are dominant	emerging new role and status for women
U.S. dominant (bipolar) challenged mainly by U.S.S.R.	multipolar world
simpler world, fewer nations, growing importance of non-national groups	more complex world, many nations, dominance of non-national groups
strategic nuclear sledgehammer	"war of the flea" (e.g., Iran)
predictable future	unpredictable future

Table 1 summarizes the factors that precondition without predetermining the following scenarios. By cleaving conditions before and after the not altogether arbitrary date of 1973, the table displays the relatively recent emergence of conditions just described.

Our attempt to be realistic has engendered our deeper appreciation for the fundamental truth that all things are connected. Interactions among the preceding factors could suddenly become critical before any one of them becomes serious enough to warn us of impending catastrophe. An example of such interaction and the complexity it introduces into the process of scenario generation is the relationship between high oil prices and flooding in Bangladesh, a link that may sound unlikely. Because the U.S. imports a great deal of oil and may be rich enough to pay for it, it has bid up the price for oil paid by poorer countries as well. Farmers in Nepal, who used to use fertilizers made from oil, must now convert to cow dung, formerly used as fuel for cooking. Firewood replaces the cow dung as fuel, forests are stripped for wood, and the topsoil erodes. The rain waters run off rather than being absorbed, rivers swell downstream, and Bangladesh is flooded in epic proportions, sweeping thousands to their death and leaving tens of thousands homeless and diseased. That such suffering stems from wasteful driving habits in America seems at first a difficult connection to accept, but the causal connections make the link real nevertheless.

In addition to uncovering causal connections that will influence the future, we explore broad structural changes that are more complex than even very long causal chains. Four assumptions guide our work in handling such structural change:

Openness to the improbable. An obvious problem with trend forecasting is that it concentrates on probable events. If an event seems highly improbable, it is considered foolish to include it in any kind of futures projection because its improbability becomes the weakest conceptual link in a series of probabilities. Nevertheless, the past two decades have witnessed many low-probability events that have had a profound influence on society. That there was only a one-in-a-million chance of the near core meltdown at Three Mile Island in no way diminishes the large impact the incident has had on nuclear regulatory processes and public concern. The only rational conclusion that one can draw from Three Mile Island and the seizure of the hostages in Iran is that low-probability events have a high probability in the course of time. Futures projections that exclude any and all low-probability events are simply sanitized futures, scrubbed, boiled, and washed. They become the least probable of all. Therefore, we have tried to place in some of the scenarios "wild cards," unforeseen events.

Power is ebbing away from central sources of control. The authors believe that people can strongly influence (not control) the future by their individual choices. It may be that the complexity of modern society prevents most individuals from formulating an image of the future sufficiently coherent to act in their own best interests. But that should not obscure the possibility that in a complex system, power may ebb from centralized sources. Just as Nietzsche indicated the shape of secular society by pronouncing the death of God, so the secular power of the Presidency is dead, signaling the end of hierarchical sources of power and control and the beginning of heterarchies, wherein power is distributed over a broad and differentiated social geography. Most ideological systems make the fundamental assumption that humankind's control over its destiny lies with the large collective institutions of public agencies and corporate hierarchies. No one denies that the behemoths of IBM and the Department of Defense have a great deal of impact on the world. But, if one asks the powerful what it feels like to be so powerful, the answer is surprising. Almost without exception they will deny their power, and not only with the purpose of escaping accountability. In the complex game played by corporations, interest groups, and regulators, each player is convinced that the power lies with the other two. All give support to the feeling of powerlessness among the so-called powerful. From time to time, one or another player may win a "victory"—a pipeline built, a pollutant banned, a new agency created — but the cost of victory gets higher all the time. The cost of litigation, the social paralysis, the declining standard of living all contribute to the growing feeling that though they are able to act, the so-called powerful cannot get what they want. If power is *the capacity to carry out reasoned intentions* — a useful definition that distinguishes human power from, say, brute *force* — then the holding of high office or position may not of itself confer real power if the institutional context of that office inhibits rather than enhances one's capacity to carry out intentions. Power has not *shifted* like some absolute quantity that must remain constant. Power has *ebbed* as each and all stymie the intentions of other agents in our highly interlocked society.

Power is exercised in a new natural environment. We confess our preference for a low-growth, decentralized future based on renewable sources of energy, one that allows a diversity of value systems and lifestyles. Yet we recognize the enduring reality of large and highly centralized institutions. Rather than pretending that everyone will share our preference, we acknowledge the historical emergence of manmade institutions that have now achieved a degree of permanence and inertia comparable to the features of the landscape and the laws of nature. For many Americans, human creations have all but replaced nature as their everyday environment. Despite the fact that those creations are the results of human choice, it does not follow that we can immediately reverse all those choices and return to a pristine natural environment. Precisely because so many of our institutions are paralyzed and their officers relatively powerless, we cannot assume that enlightened policies will issue immediately in beneficial changes. To the extent that many of our institutions have gone beyond and sometimes subverted the intentions that created them, they now constitute a neo-natural realm of impacts and forces, not a human world of reasoned intentions. The proper goal for human power, therefore, does not include moving all the mountains of our modern neo-nature. Instead, a more rational stance toward this new environment would mimic an ecological sensitivity toward nature. We can carve out livable spaces within the new landscape without trying to radically alter the landscape to conform to our sometimes nostalgic preferences. Real power can accrue to people who understand the limits of human control over nature, old and new, and who therefore measure their preferences against an understanding of what can and cannot be accomplished in a day or a decade.

Attention to changes in perceptions and belief systems. Most futurist research assumes that people change primarily in response to events, and that history unfolds on the basis of objective facts. We assume that people change for many reasons. We have concentrated a great deal of our attention on the study of how and when people do change their values and behavior. While large and deterministic forces will, we acknowledge, affect us all, the influence that emanates from the ways in which individuals perceive the world is equally powerful.

The seven scenarios we finally chose represent most clearly the spectrum of divergent futures possible within the next twenty years. They explore the most optimistic forecasts of the driving trends, as well as the most pessimistic. Table 2 describes each of the driving trends and their various dispositions.

Table 2
Driving Trends

ENERGY

Continued high growth. The overall historical trend of high growth (2-4 percent) in energy consumption continues.

Controlled growth. There is real growth but at a self-imposed limit of between 1-2 percent.

Unsuccessful high growth. Continued high growth is attained for a certain period but is then disrupted by severe supply problems resulting in a rapid net decline in supplies.

Zero or declining growth. The growth rate in energy consumption is level or slightly less (0 to -3 percent).

CLIMATE

Favorable climate. The trend from 1890-1960 of generally constant, good, and predictable weather is resumed. From year to year, the weather pattern aids expanding agricultural production.

Variable climate. From year to year, the climate is relatively unpredictable, swinging from good to bad. In some years, the weather conditions for agriculture are generally favorable. In others, drought, untimely rain, or shortened growing seasons are experienced.

Worsening. The trend from 1960-1980 of cooler weather and shifting, hence unpredictable weather is continued. In most years, droughts, untimely rain, shortened growing season, or other weather-related calamities become common.

FOOD

Moderate prices/no shortage. The "ideal" situation wherein food production stays sufficiently ahead of demand. Sufficient energy supplies insure adequate distribution of food to most peoples.

High price/no shortage. There are a number of ways in which food can soar in cost without there being any real shortage: e.g., rapid increase in energy prices, a moderate degree of adverse weather, high food exports to enhance balance of payments deficits, more affluence leading to higher consumption of proteinaceous and convenience foods, and greater population here and abroad.

High prices/shortages. This assumes that a combination of circumstances, domestic or international, creates conditions in which the food supply is short and very expensive. Such a condition might be very bad weather conditions combined with an energy shortage.

ECONOMY

Conventional. A slow to moderately growing economy with intermittent, mild recessions and adjustments. Single-digit inflation.

Volatile. A rapidly changing economy wherein short periods of spurting growth are followed by sharp reversals and counter trends. Sharp inflationary trends.

Declining. Stagnant economy that slowly contracts in overall output and productivity.

Bust. An economic mini-boom that is accompanied by double-digit inflation leads to a deflationary or an inflationary collapse.

VALUES

Achievement values. Emphasis on material possessions, status, fame, affluence, and outward achievement—recognition, growth, bigness, and competition. Tendencies include mechanistic, materialistic, highly individualistic, secular, centralized, hierarchical, patriarchal, scientistic, empirical.

Survival values. Survival values include all of the above values but are the result when those values cannot be realized or attained. When a materialistic culture cannot obtain enough goods, the consequences are frustration, dogged endurance with an emphasis on personal security, and survival, intolerance, and conflict.

Frugal values. Self-imposed restrictions on consumption because of need to simplify life or tendency to be frugal; emphasis on flexibility, cooperation, and a "man in nature" evolutionary ethic. Other tendencies congruent with these are heterarchical, matriarchal, naturalistic, decentralist, humanistic.

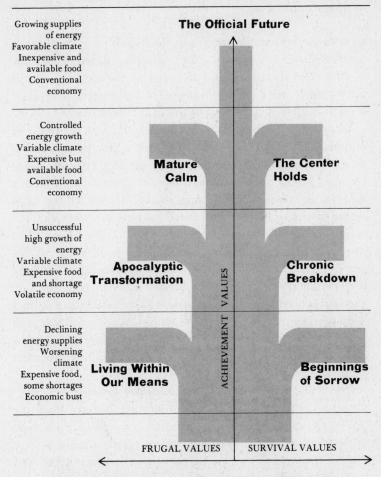

Growing supplies of energy Favorable climate Inexpensive and available food Conventional economy	**The Official Future** ↑	
Controlled energy growth Variable climate Expensive but available food Conventional economy	**Mature Calm**	**The Center Holds**
Unsuccessful high growth of energy Variable climate Expensive food and shortage Volatile economy	**Apocalyptic Transformation**	**Chronic Breakdown**
Declining energy supplies Worsening climate Expensive food, some shortages Economic bust	**Living Within Our Means**	**Beginnings of Sorrow**

ACHIEVEMENT VALUES

← FRUGAL VALUES | SURVIVAL VALUES →

The Seven Scenarios: Tracks Plotted Against Value Orientations and Differing States of the Other Driving Trends

The diagram above portrays the pattern of divergence of the seven scenarios in terms of various constellations of driving trends and values. The vertical vector in the center represents Achievement Values, one of the three basic value systems as outlined in the table of Driving Trends. That vertical vector also represents an impetus to achieve the Official Future. The right and left arms of the bottom axis represent the two other value systems, Survival Values and Frugal Values. Scenarios placed toward any of these three directions are influenced by the respective sets of values; the nearer a scenario is placed to a given axis, the greater is the influence of that set of values in that scenario.

Our approach opens itself to the obvious criticism that it leaves out many other possibilities or combinations. For instance, what would happen if energy were abundant but food critically short? Or what would happen if there were a tri-modal split among values rather than a shift from one to another. We did not try to escape these possibilities, but instead have created what we think is the palette necessary for creating other possible futures. The seven offered contain the basic elements that would occur in most other combinations of driving trends, and are therefore the basic colors of the spectrum. There is, however, one pigment missing, and that is black: nuclear war. Although we think it is a distinct and awesomely terrible possibility, we choose not to include it in any of the scenarios because it is the end of the future as we know it. In Part Three, however, we discuss the possibility of nuclear conflict.

Other uncertainties enter the scenarios in ways that supplement the possibilities without following directly from the driving trends. Factors such as the future of our political alliances or the climatic impact of rising levels of carbon dioxide involve degrees of complexity we are barely able to understand and even less able to control. Further, there are the accidents of history: earthquakes, typhoons, gold strikes, and who knows what.

The message that comes across most strongly in traversing these seven scenarios is the degree to which we must face and deal with uncertainty and ambiguity when thinking about the future. Our purpose is not to eliminate the uncertainty, uncomfortable as it may be, but rather to explore its dimensions. To the degree to which this exercise succeeds as an exploratory venture, it is more of a heuristic process than a predictive one. The results we are seeking are modes of perception rather than methods of prognostication.

Each of the seven scenarios that follow should be considered as an alternative image of the future, to be read as a history, a contradiction that is intentional. By looking back at the future we grant ourselves a perspective that is difficult to achieve when looking ahead. A history never covers all events but focuses instead on those issues and forces that shaped the period. Histories and scenarios alike try to paint a comprehensive picture that also reveals the nature of the times.

The first scenario, The Official Future, largely contradicts many of the thirteen conditions we earlier described as elements that must be dealt with in any future. The point is, we may be wrong. The Republican platform committee may have the most accurate picture of the future. Suppose that many of the current trends in energy, climate, food, and the economy are not accurate when projected. Suppose the exponential curves of computer models have bewitched us into a totally false malaise, and that all of the talk of lowered expectations and income is merely a siren's song luring us toward the shoals of pessimism. What if the future is richer, more prosperous, and more lavish than we ever dreamed? What if we are on the verge of $50,000 per year average salaries, increasing knowledge, and startling breakthroughs in technology? What if our greatest achievements lie just ahead? The first scenario, The Official Future, explores what our lives might be like.

PART TWO
SEVEN SCENARIOS
FOR THE
EIGHTIES AND
NINETIES

Chapter III
The Official Future

Technological triumph sums up the Official Future. American power is ascendant. While the instabilities and inequities of the world have not ended, the plight of the world's poorer nations improves markedly as a result of U.S. leadership. The spread of Soviet ideology is checked. At home people are optimistic and satisfied with the "American experiment." More people are more affluent than ever. The quality of life thrives on a quantity of goods and services undreamt of by earlier generations. Higher education, improved health care, and vacation travel become available to a higher percentage of the population. More personal computers and Cuisinarts wind up in the hands of the middle classes. The race for economic success remains active because the prizes remain appealing and attainable.

Along with burgeoning technology, increased productivity, smoothly functioning world trade, and widespread affluence, we encounter rapid environmental deterioration, rising crime rates, and restrictions on personal freedom hidden behind the wealth. Nevertheless, in the Official Future, people gladly trade clean air and water for a new car or some comparable commodity.

I N RETROSPECT, it is obvious that the nadir of post-war America occurred during the Carter administration, specifically the hostage crisis in Iran in 1979 and 1980. After the Reagan election, America got tough. The momentum changed. No-nonsense government budgets contrasted with resurgent corporate spending and investment. By 1984, American economic growth was 4 percent per year, second only to the Japanese. The sense that America had been too soft too long pervaded domestic issues where conservatives swept away volumes of environmental regulations and obstacles. By tying energy to national security, the government was able to push a broad program involving nuclear, oil shale, LNG, and coal through the Congress. As in the fifties, the country once again became pro-nuclear, pro-energy, and pro-consumption.

The eighties witnessed a restored sense of achievement, supported by a growing sense of mastery over the physical world. Successes in technology renewed America's confidence in its ability to determine its destiny. The supply-side economists did not end inflation, but they clearly showed that the economy could be rationally changed for the better by thinking human beings. Productivity rose, as did savings, income, and output. The triumph of the sciences scattered the ranks of the doubters and Cassandras, while it made the soft-spoken conservatives of the establishment seem prescient in their quiet faith in progress.

America began to reap the harvest of technological research performed during the two prior decades. Mass production and miniaturization of electronics brought fully interactive computers to most of the populace. Terminals were routinely put into new houses and apartments as standard equipment. Teenagers strapped wafer-sized computers with the power of the old IBM 360 onto their arms. Experimentation in computer research moved toward direct lobal implants respondent to remote transmission devices hidden on the body. Technicians' capabilities for programming people's pleasures and feelings ran ahead of psychologists' evaluations of the consequences of mood modification.

While biological applications of recombinant DNA proliferated rapidly, genetic engineers opened new vistas by designing microbes that could alter industrial devices and materials: alloys and ceramics with completely new properties; crystals for new forms of electronic circuits; new fibers, plastics, and lubricants. Miniaturization in medicine resulted in electrocardiogram monitors that were embedded in clothing and could automatically

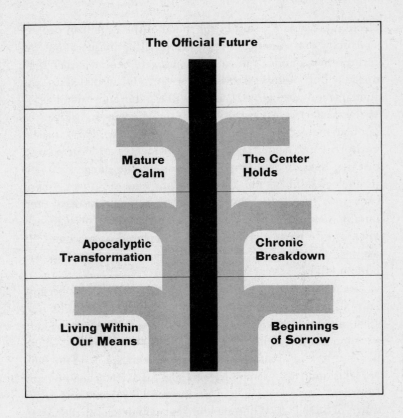

The Official Future

Mature Calm

The Center Holds

Apocalyptic Transformation

Chronic Breakdown

Living Within Our Means

Beginnings of Sorrow

signal the patient and medical authorities if a heart attack or seizure was imminent. In California, an electronics company developed an artificial pancreas (PanKreaz) that monitored sugar in the bloodstream and released insulin as needed.

PanKreaz had hardly been on the market a year when the University of Chicago announced the first successful cloning and implantation of a pancreas into a diabetic patient. Within months, organ after organ was cloned, and the clamor for replacement parts was almost frenzied. When the University of California in Los Angeles revealed that fetuses had been successfully grown in vitrio, Congress took legislative steps to regulate and license parthenogenesis.

These dramatic breakthroughs in medicine, biology, and

electronics overlaid a shift in the mood of the American people. Polls show that Americans once again felt optimistic about the future, that America's worst problems were behind rather than ahead. But history shows otherwise. It seems that the fundamental change was not in the nature or number of problems facing America, but in the manner in which the population faced them. High energy and food prices, environmental degradation, rising incidences of degenerative diseases, spasms of international tension, the dangers of new technologies — these and other problems were the prices Americans paid for civilization. Certain cities were unhealthy and unsafe. Certain parts of the environment were permanently lost. Certain parts of the body were replaced or mechanically assisted. Certain parts of society were maladjusted. This was normal.

And to the relief of many, prosperity once again became normal. Real income increased 40 percent between 1981 and 1990, although distribution of the increase was uneven. There were ten million millionaires by the end of the decade. Median home prices in desirable suburbs had climbed to $400,000. No-frills compact automobiles were sold for $15,000 and up. The "average" family of four had an income of $95,000 and a net worth of $570,000. While the indigent population of the urban homeless increased tenfold during the eighties, the common sight of bag ladies and bums did not dampen the enthusiasm with which Americans cut back on taxes, social welfare programs, and government spending. Instead, attention shifted to the more pressing concerns of terrorism — at home in the form of youth gangs and abroad as political acts — as well as national security, and the search for resources.

What characterized America's approach to problems was its doggedness in looking for symptomatic cures while ignoring the long-term consequences of its actions. The massive shift in energy production from oil to coal produced a considerable rise in lung-related diseases, which were in turn countered by lung cloning, implantation, cancer insurance, and air infiltration systems in urban housing. The crime wave that had begun after World War II continued unabated, and was carried out increasingly by the young with cruelty, irrationality, and perversion. Security businesses grew into giant industries, private armies of the night became common throughout suburbia, while behavior modification and aversion therapy became increasingly acceptable within the prison system.

America became richer, but not all Americans became rich. The labor unions polarized sharply as the clear distinction between labor-intensive and capital-intensive industries created broad disparities in paychecks. In 1988, the Garment Workers (ILGWU) argued for $9 an hour in their contract talks, while the Atomic and Chemical Workers Union walked out for three months after rejecting a pay package offering them $46 an hour.

The labor shortage that began in the mid-eighties hastened rapidly the full integration of women into the workplace, producing a new type of sexual arrogance known as "machisma." While many women brought sensibilities and concerns to business that made commerce more human, many more succumbed to the power of position. With male subordinates in abundance, female executives could play the field with an aggressively flirtatious style that echoed male chauvinism.

The growth of the technological society demanded better schooling, a need that was met by private institutions. While the progeny of the technocratic elite became ever more literate, "technological illiteracy" placed growing numbers of less fortunate youth on the wrong end of the information economy. With the public schools closely approximating detention centers, the United States educational system began to resemble the Russian system — 2 percent of the population received the best education while the balance fell behind. The disparities in knowledge and skills resulted in highly skewed incomes. The ability to gather, control, disseminate, and market information clearly distinguished those who were rapidly benefiting from the system from those who were merely coping.

The astounding transformation to an information society was

accompanied by a corresponding loss of privacy. Despite denials by the government, the computerization of government records, combined with the sharing of private and public data bases, meant former privileges were accompanied by unprecedented surveillance. But most people accepted the institutional monitoring of individual habits as a small price to pay for the conveniences.

By the end of the eighties, the ubiquitous computer terminal stared at everyone everywhere. With virtually all financial services available by computer at supermarkets, department stores, and train stations, the distinction between the Bank of America and Sears, Roebuck practically disappeared. At the bank, you could call up thousands of purveyors on a CRT and order goods directly while charging them to your bank account. At Sears, you could get a loan, sell options, buy stocks, or add T-bills to your Keogh account — also on a CRT. No longer did it matter "what" you were doing with your money. What mattered was your record, how well you understood the electronic system of money transfers, and the income flow that was automatically transferred by employers and investments to your account. As money changed from paper to magnetic signals, available credit was largely used by the affluent and technologically literate. The information poor fumbled with paper money, rudimentary banking services, and lack of comprehension. With little access to credit at reasonable terms, they fell further behind economically, which finally raised the question of credit access as a human rights issue by 1990.

The inevitable result of a sophisticated society was that its progeny should learn early what the rules of the game were supposed to be. Juvenile rights were first taken up by the "Six Teens" of Canton, Ohio, who, after being arrested for minor curfew and drug violations, sued both the police and the state under the First, Fifth, and Fourteenth Amendments, citing specifically the denial of the right to assemble, denial of due process, and discrimination in violation of the equal protection clause.

As the case escalated, it attracted enormous media attention, in part because the "Six" had an almost scriptlike ability to act in a disarming manner. Neat, well dressed, and on the whole successful students at their own Lincoln High School, the Six contended that just as laws against minorities and women were found to be both unconstitutional and unwarranted, the laws controlling the behavior and discipline of minors were archaic, illegal, in violation of the Constitution, and reflected a prejudice against youth that was self-fulfilling in very much the way that sexist attitudes could reinforce a woman's negative self-image. Although they ultimately lost their case in the Supreme Court, they won over the country's youth, many of whom boycotted schools, institutions, corporations, and homelife on their contention that these organizations and institutions were exploiting and discriminating against youth in overt and subtle ways. Some states repealed curfew laws, lowered the legal definition of minor from age eighteen to sixteen, and restricted the rights of juvenile authorities. Teens demanded that youth sit on police advisory boards and on the boards of companies that sold products to youth such as CBS (records) and Levi Strauss. Juvenile courts had youth advisors, high schools had students attending faculty meetings, and many youths refused calisthenics and physical education courses until their overweight teachers joined them on the field for pushups. On the whole, the movement was healthy because it created a dialogue where little existed previously. With the repeal of minor laws, juveniles faced adult courts and penalties, and often the severe judgments seemed too much for the public to bear. Virtually every one of the Six entered some form of public life including Nicholette Bonner, who became the youngest woman ever elected to Congress in 1998.

The exponential rate of social change generated great resistance from some traditional sectors of society. Featherbedding kept supernumeraries on the job at declining industries, government bureaucracies, and failing institutions. While public schools grimly hung on with blackboards and books, advanced

41

corporations employed holographic visualization to train employees for new jobs. While the old automobile manufacturing centers of the northeast decayed, the Houston/L.A. corridor boomed. While executives communicated with wrist telephones between appointments, a radical ecology movement protested violently against microwave proliferation and claimed that it was tantamount to electronic pollution by the large corporations. (They pointed to the 500 percent increase in cataract operations as evidence of the problem.)

By 1990, the term "average family" had no meaning. It is said that things disappear for which there is no vocabulary — and so it was with families. Reproduction continued, at declining levels from earlier decades, but the family unit continued to disintegrate. Both parents worked in 80 percent of the homes, but average families stayed together only six years. A minority of children lived with both parents. After the demise of the family came the disappearance of youth. In 1990, twelve years was the median age for sexual maturation. The increasing frequency of pre-teen abortions bore out Herman Kahn's earlier prediction that the main problem facing America toward the end of the twentieth century would be degeneracy rather than prosperity.

If by 1990 choices were already too broad and life too complex, society was hardly prepared for the wave of change that has swept us up until today. In 1993, the Japanese stunned the world by launching the first solar power generating station, an elaborate skein of aluminized membranes and graphite threads that unfolded mechanically in the sky to equal an area one-half the size of Manhattan. It beamed back 75 megawatts of energy to receiving stations on Kyushu and prompted crash accelerations of American and French programs. By 1998, ten 3,000 megawatt stations had been launched. As each new man-made star rose in the heavens, people all over the earth — not just poets, lovers, and astronomers — howled at the fact that even the night sky was now a human artifact. Year after year, square moons were placed in the microwave belt of the night, removing forever the view of the stars alone. And year after year, bird populations were decimated around receiving stations as the microwaves killed or damaged flocks.

By the nineties, bio-technologies had the theoretical ability to create host diseases that could wipe out whole species of insects and vermin. With the ability to wipe out the fly at our fingertips, nervous speculation among entomologists and ecologists revolved around the nature of the decision, and the magnitude of its consequences.

In media, broadcasting changed to narrowcasting, interactive cable networks that allowed viewers to select from over a hundred programs at any given time. Mass delivery of information by networks and large publishers catered to a shrinking share of the audience. People called up news and information on their TV via the computer. While some learned more, more knew less about the world. Sensitivity to world affairs met rough competition from the onslaught of sexuality on private networks. But more important, fewer citizens were sharing similar information. This situation brought about a highly diverse and erratic quality to voting patterns, polls, and decision-making. Imparting information to the citizenry became so difficult and competitive that in 1994 the government finally opened its own network of stations.

The dark side of the disappearance of the family became more obvious with the rise in suicides among the middle-aged and senescent. Small groups formed societies in which they were taught to voluntarily terminate their lives, a movement which was fought and argued about with no clear resolution. For the middle-aged, the cause was the loss of meaning, made more illusive by wealth, goods, and sated desires. For the elderly, it was loss of connection. With no families to provide emotional support, many of the elderly chose to depart early.

Internationally, America made great strides in forming a transnational community in North America. Canada, Mexico, and the U.S. joined together to form the North American Industry and Technology Alliance (NAITA), an international consortium for the exchange, export, and development of energy, transportation, agriculture, and communications. Due to the labor shortage of the mid-eighties, the U.S. relaxed its ineffective restrictions on Mexican immigration. Following Canada's harrowing experience of near Balkanization by its several provinces, a new internationalist government in Ottawa reversed its opposition to U.S. involvement and welcomed the meliorating effect of American investment and cultural homogenization. While North Americans learned more Spanish, Mexico improved the flow of natural gas and oil to the U.S.

Good weather, which had temporarily receded during the late sixties and seventies, returned by the late eighties. The effort by NAITA to stimulate North American food production on a transnational level was spectacularly successful and made it the OPEC of food. Mexican production of urea, ammonium sulfate, and pesticides, along with enormous water projects, brought hundreds of thousands of acres of Mexican land into full production. Mexico became the fruit and vegetable basket of wintertime North America.

American success in agriculture, coupled with its ability to meet the challenges posed by energy and resources, caused a marked shift away from socialist and Marxist sentiments in the Third World. With the heavily centralized Soviet system foundering in its own restrictiveness, the have-not nations thought twice before allowing Russian participation in their development. The Western economic machine was far outperforming its Soviet counterpart, and the gap between capitalist and socialist nations was widening.

America's increasing prosperity encouraged undeveloped countries to believe that they would be able to replicate the economic miracles of Brazil and Korea. Most of them saw coexistence with America as critical to their well-being. Countries that had earlier attacked and even nationalized American assets did an about-face and wooed multinational corporations. Because it was critical to development, capital spoke louder than political ideology. The rising relative affluence of Third World countries did more than any other single factor to lower birth rates, and it now appears that world population may stabilize within forty years.

In January 1996, the world learned that the era of United States expansion was not over. In a series of carefully timed launches, four space shuttles carried into earth orbit the components for Skybase I — nicknamed Asimov for the science fiction writer. The announced purpose of the base was research on space construction and manufacturing, astronomy, earth resources, and weather. But the secrecy enveloping Asimov seemed to confirm the presence of laser and possibly particle beam weapons in space, further consolidating American hegemony through weaponry and defensive systems.

Skybase I also provided the final link within the global communications system that began with Comsat. Unnoticed by most was the fact that it was the instant economic interaction provided by satellite communication that most contributed to world peace. With all governments and banks fully interlinked, the vulnerability of the international economic system to disruption was evident to all — and repugnant to all. Untoward activities of a single government could be instantly punished by the world financial community, which became in effect a shadow governing body. This control of the flow of capital and information worldwide shifted power away from governmental institutions in the public sector to concentrations of wealth in the private sector.

In the U.S., the concept of an information economy became dramatically evident in the financial world. A company called Relative Economics developed a computer model of market behavior that worked so precisely that they were able to turn a $250,000 investment into $4 billion during a seven-year period. Because its very size began to "contaminate" the market, another company, Trans Data Resources, tapped the RE program, fed it into their own model, and developed a new program to do precisely what RE had done so successfully: make a long series of successful, highly leveraged trades on many markets simultaneously. TDR's success stimulated other cybernetic models of

45

market behavior. In a short time, success in the stock market was largely confined to a small, highly secretive group of people with vast computers, sophisticated programs, and huge amounts of liquidity. Producers such as farmers, mining companies, and corporations protested market manipulation by so few, but none could counter the argument that these new trading companies were engaged in "free markets." Their effective monopoly consisted of their temporary edge in computer modeling. As that knowledge becomes widespread, the market is returning to some semblance of normalcy or "efficiency" as economists describe it. This return to an efficient market involves recognition of the extent to which information has itself become a commodity, as reflected by the fact that several of the companies like RE and TDR sold stock and are traded in turn, creating still another wrinkle in what has become a supremely complex information economy.

With the information economy having shattered the old patterns of commuting and centralization, many people work at home or in specially constructed "cells." The rise of "electronic narcissism" is accompanied by stories about programmers who rarely leave their CRTs or homes. Even with the advent of the small, pamphlet-sized terminal, the electronic troglodytes remain sequestered in their grottoes. The electronic monks differ from "software jocks," the young professionals who make $300,000 to $400,000 a year and drive luxuriant mobile homes jammed with computing and telecommunications equipment. Their specialty is programming the giant Cray sub-micron computers leased by utility companies, public transportation agencies, and banks. They usually burn out before age twenty-five, hence their high wages, their use of highly paid agents, and their subsequent employment as endorsers of various software packages.

Efficiency has become the watchword of society. People arrive on time to meetings. Promptness and precision are the universally accepted norm. Careless errors have become a rarity. And efficiency has led to success in human interactions as well as in production. There are differences of opinion about how to handle emotions. Some maintain that emotions have their own rhythms and purposes, not to be interrupted by the demands of daily schedules or psychotropic drugs. The anti-drug contingent starts the day by "cleaning house," a series of carefully developed techniques extracted from the now defunct human potential movement of the seventies. So while the pharmacological group takes the appropriate pills to create desired moods, the Interpersonal Dynamics Techniques adherents are already at work practicing. But either way, by the time people get to their jobs, most of the work force is alert and ready to go. The debate over means is not so much resolved as tabled, since both drugs and IDTs have proven to be equally efficient. Both sides say time will tell.

Meanwhile, the high whine of the economy running at peak performance is a pleasure to the ears of engineers. While electrical, chemical, nuclear, and social engineers have reason to be proud, psychologists, still reluctant to be called "psychic engineers," feel no cause for joy in their incapacity to prevent occasional mental disorders. People keep breaking down as unpredictably as ever — perhaps, more often. It is as if madness descends at random to pick its victims. Such attacks remain disquieting to those who watch with dismay as one of their own number suddenly disappears from the temporarily shattered calm that characterizes the normal. But symptoms, once evident, can be treated even if the onset remains unpredictable. And efficiency always picks up again.

Around the world, there are signs of enormous impoverishment of the global commons. While America continues to grow materially, firewood is nonexistent in parts of Africa and the Indian subcontinent. Coal exports helped relieve some of the suffering, but the need for wood is so great that America is cutting and exploiting her own noneconomically productive forests. Although the shortage of fuel has provided a much needed export industry for New England, relief agencies contend that the hardwoods rarely get to the people in need.

Water begins to look like the scarce commodity of the next

century. Those with foresight enough to have purchased tracts of water rights in Colorado have become "aquannaires," pumping and selling water at $3 per ton, close to the price of oil in 1970. At the same time, salinization and ground water depletion in California have put tens of thousands of acres out of production, and these problems raise serious questions about the future of the San Joaquin Valley.

Desertification threatens to eliminate half of the Australian wheat production within the next ten years unless remedies are found. The Sahel and midwestern United States are also badly affected. The Serengeti is being chopped up into farms, causing havoc with the migratory patterns of wildebeest, antelope, giraffe, and springbok.

But the good news is that the third industrial revolution is about to begin. With the launching next year in 2001 of Skybase III, construction will begin on the trillion-dollar project to build a prototypical space colony in L-5. Much of the industrialized world, recognizing the deteriorating condition of our planet, is placing great hope in the accelerated development of this long-delayed project. It is predicted that earth can be a net importer of resources by 2060, and that a reversal of the degradation of earth's carrying capacity can begin then.

Our work shows that in order for the Official Future to be realized, there must be adequate and affordable energy, a calm and steady global climate, a stable growth economy, and no food or resource shortages. Blessed with those conditions and the dominance of achievement values, the Official Future might be a plausible scenario for the next twenty years. The Official Future assumes that the world is basically in good shape, that the recent past was aberrant, and that the decades ahead will be times of unrestrained success. By placing this scenario first we do not mean to suggest that it represents the best future. It does mean, as shown in the diagram on page 29, that there are relatively benign conditions in terms of driving trends that combine with conventional, established values.

In the Official Future, American pursuit of material abundance and world dominance provokes rapid change accompany rapid growth. The impact and direction of that accompanying change are not as predictable as its pursuit would imply. The dominant mentality driving the Official Future does not include within its purview an underlying sense of consequences, nor does it contain the sensitivity required to foresee the detailed impact of new technologies, rapid environmental transformation, or new social configurations. While planners project particular changes as chronological improvements, interactions among many changes produce exponential growth rates adding problems to our successes.

This failure to appreciate complex and interactive consequences is partly a function of people's faith in officialdom: despite visible deterioration of parts of the environment, despite exponential growth rates that threaten imminent shortages of resources, an abiding confidence in technical expertise allows most individuals to proceed with business as usual. "Someone must be minding the store."

Because individuals behave as though individual decisions are not important to the course of collective history, they pursue short-term goals of private wealth and security. If all goes well, if the weather is good, if world leaders keep the peace, if energy, food, and natural resources are found and distributed in sufficient quantities, then we may just teeter across the tightrope of the Official Future for another two decades. But there are so many ways to go wrong, any one of which can throw us off this perilous balance. And the great danger is just this: if what motivates the Official Future is a faith in officialdom, then the first lurch toward systematic imbalance is likely to produce a call for stronger leadership. Our next scenario shows what happens when the values and mentality of the Official Future meet with less benign conditions.

Table 3
Statistics: The Official Future

	1980	2000
World Population (in millions)	4,500	6,797
U.S. Population (in millions)	226	268
World GNP (in billions)	7,000	17,353
U.S. GNP (in billions)	2,600	4,602
U.S. Per Capita Disposable Income	8,100	11,900
U.S. Per Capita Consumption Expenditures	7,400	10,700
Average World Energy Prices ($/bbl crude)	35	50
Energy Consumption (quads)	78	123
Energy Supply by Source (quads)		
Domestic Oil	20	23
Imported Oil	15	22
Shale Oil	0	3
Natural Gas	20	19
Coal	17	40
Conventional Nuclear	3	10
Nuclear Breeder	0	1
Solar, Hydropower, and Other	3	5
Percentage of Income Spent On		
Housing	21	19
Food	21	20
Clothing	8	7
Medical Care	10	13
Transportation	15	13

Note: 1 quad = 10^{15} Btu/yr; all dollar figures are in 1980 dollars.

Table 4
Trends: The Official Future

Countries growing economically: *

Brazil	Korea
Malaysia	Indonesia
Nigeria	Philippines
South Africa	Taiwan
Mexico	People's Republic of China

Countries contracting economically: **

Cuba	Poland	Jamaica
Nicaragua	Tanzania	

Countries standing still:

Great Britain	Italy	India
Iran	Turkey	

Occupations which are rapidly growing in demand:

Programmers	Security engineers
Electronics engineers	Technical managers
Circuit designers	Repair/maintenance
Bioengineers	technicians
Behavioral designers	Medical technicians
Military officers	Communication specialists

Occupations which are shrinking in demand:

Farmhands	Filing clerks
Assembly line workers	Politicians
Machinists	Fishermen
Cashiers/tellers	Short-order cooks

Businesses which are growing:

Communication	Bio-industry
Health industry	Specialty chemicals
Electronics	Nuclear power
Aerospace/weaponry	Entertainment

Businesses which are contracting:

Textiles	Commodity chemicals
Apparel	Handtools
Automobiles	Metal forming

*Top 10 percent in growth of GNP 1995-2000
**Bottom 5 percent in growth of GNP 1995-2000

Chapter IV

The Center Holds

The Center Holds begins precisely in the same manner as the Official Future. The eighties start out bullish and aggressive. America is militarily assertive abroad and forceful at home in solving its energy problems. Technology after technology issues forth from corporate America promising answers to present and future problems. But shortly thereafter, America is confounded with problems. Energy supplies are suddenly reduced, the economy stops growing, and social unrest is exacerbated by rising food prices caused by an erratic climate.

In response, the survivalist prophets crow with righteousness and prematurely pat themselves on the back for their prescience in calling America's fate. In the end, the survivalists are proven wrong. Instead of a devolving economy and society, the large multinational corporations combine their forces with big government to restore systems. The new system is highly centralized and more authoritarian. A conservatively packed Supreme Court interprets the First Amendment increasingly narrowly. As conformity becomes the passport to success, the system becomes rigid and intolerant. Science is evermore the handmaiden of government, with increasing amounts of research funded by the central government. And technology, buoyed by its successes in curing the fundamental energy problems of the eighties, becomes government's major tool for collecting all of the pertinent data about society needed to ensure that the nation could not break down again as it almost did in the eighties.

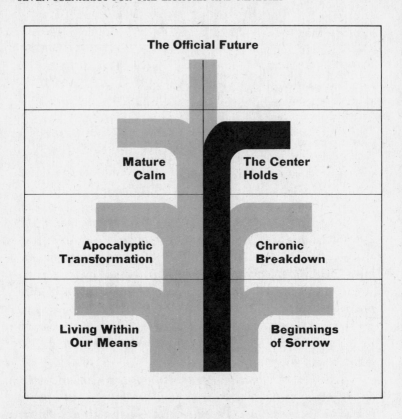

The Official Future

Mature
Calm

The Center
Holds

Apocalyptic
Transformation

Chronic
Breakdown

Living Within
Our Means

Beginnings
of Sorrow

THE SURPRISING EVENTS of 1983 were, in retrospect, entirely predictable. The most obvious problem was the manner in which America had dealt with the rising price of energy, to wit, by simply issuing more and more U.S. dollars, which in turn prompted further ratcheting up of oil prices. The oil-consuming nations confronted the declining value of the dollar in the spring of 1984 when OPEC nations announced and unified behind $75-per-barrel oil, combined with a 25 percent reduction in production.

Despite the hawkish screaming from the floor of the U.S. Senate, the *Wall Street Journal* pointed out in an op-ed article that the rises in energy price were the Arabs' only way to keep abreast of the continued devaluation of the American dollar, a problem that the American consumer was not coping with. Although inflation had exceeded 20 percent for the first time in 1983, the 1984 price hike drove it up further, and produced wild gyrations in the prices of gold, commodities, and bonds. The economy started to plunge and it seemed clear from the sell-off in stocks that this recession was going to be the biggest since the depression. Cries for wage and price controls extended far beyond the unions. For the first time, Republicans and heads of corporations joined the chorus for strong government control of the economy.

Despite everyone's worst fears, the great recession did not dip as deeply as feared. Unemployment shot up to 12 percent, but once again the seemingly indomitable American economy stood firm in the face of doomsayers. Nevertheless, inflation and unemployment slowly worsened. For the first time in post-war history, there was no immediate sign of a recovery. Following an overall drop of 20 percent in production and GNP, the economic indicators stabilized and steadied.

For the middle and working classes, the rapid economic decline created a sense of failure, even self-hate. The need for scapegoats to explain the dilemma in which America found itself was nicely met by anyone who did not conform to narrow definitions of what was "American." The first wave of resentment targeted extreme lifestyles and crime. Gangs of youths dressed in urban cowboy gear began to raid gay neighborhoods, smash windows, slash tires, and terrorize people. Out-of-town gangs cruised through large cities and attacked any evidence of non-conformity. Ku Klux Klan and Neo-Nazi activity surged in rural and southern areas. Synagogues were attacked and Jews were baited.

As the economy continued to show no signs of recovery, the malaise infused politics, in particular the House, where a "revitalized" Un-American Activities Committee was formed and began hearings across the country. In televised and well-publicized sessions, Chairman Freeman Caruthers subpoenaed and grilled representatives from a wide variety of spiritual, political, and social movements. Members of anti-nuclear groups, "new age" religions, Oriental disciplines, gay men's and women's organizations, drug magazine editors, rock 'n roll groups, the movie industry (Jane Fonda, Robert Redford), and environmental groups were lumped under the rubric of "these people" by Chairman Caruthers. "These people" were asked why they had conspired to prevent the true moral voice of the people from being heard, why they tried to stop economic growth, what their motives were in accusing big business of deceit, sham, and fraud. Caruthers asked a woman leader of the Clamshell Alliance how many black and red men she had slept with. He asked gay men if they thought of the Bible when they were fornicating. He wanted to know why Jane Fonda spent her money and "good looks" trying to delude American youth to socialist and anarchist ends. He wanted to know if practicers of TM had prayed to God Almighty for guidance before turning to the heathen religions. What would have been absurdly deplorable a decade prior was thrust righteously into American living rooms. The expected protest against such demagoguery was absent.

Politicians, judges, high office holders and executives who spoke out against the witch hunts and repression were sometimes jailed for drug or sex violations. The Lieutenant Governor of Connecticut was "entrapped" into a gay liaison and humiliated into resigning. A high-ranking officer of a bank was "found" in a depraved state high on drugs. Whispering campaigns, firings, trumped-up charges, character assassination, and economic pressures began to eat and tear away at resistance to HUAC. Families who resisted the committee were broken down by unexplained arson, public derision, and harassment. Liberal students saw their government loans withdrawn. Union members attacked the ghettoes of Hispanics and Puerto Ricans. Deportations filled the court dockets. Doctors accused of performing abortions faced increasingly hostile juries. In several locales, school boards acceded to the creationist movement and quietly removed the Darwinian theory of evolution from the curriculum. Religious intolerance extended beyond the Bible

Belt into some of the new-age groups, where defensive paranoia gave way to a fortress mentality that brooked no dissent inside their shaky gates. Since a casual interest in Oriental religions no longer seemed worth the risk, those who wanted to pursue non-Christian devotions found themselves forced into secrecy and esotericism. Some cults rivaled HUAC with their own tribunals.

During the 1988 Presidential campaign, both candidates ran on the same platform. For those who saw a collapsing economy, tighter management was the answer. For those who saw diversity (moral degeneration) as the source of disorder, simpleminded patriotism and a call for uniformity were the answer. For those who saw lawlessness as the problem, tighter social control was the answer. Both candidates were paternal and strong — men that "you can trust in these trying times." Both had been carefully managed by those who knew precisely how to read the mood of the voters.

For the American President-elect in 1989, the stress of campaigning had been overtaxing. On the eve of his inauguration he died of a massive heart attack. The next morning, the Chief Justice of the Supreme Court swore in the Vice-President-elect, a former professional athlete, a staunch conservative, and as everyone was quick to point out, a "born leader."

The President quickly took control. During his first one hundred days in office he surprised both his supporters and detractors. Wage and price controls were immediately instituted by executive order. He issued strict currency controls for both tourists and importers. Legislation that put American money back on the gold standard collapsed the world market for gold and sent the American dollar soaring in international trading. Hoarders tried to sell their gold as it became obvious that the speculative bubble buoying up gold would be destroyed if America had a gold-backed dollar.

Price controls were rigid. No industry or business could raise prices without a permit. Infractions were dealt with quickly and harshly. All consumer commodities were price fixed — bread at $2.12 per pound, milk at $4.40 per gallon, and gasoline at $5.50

per gallon. Unions could not strike for wages higher than those allowed by the Wage and Price Commission. Those that did were sued, their leaders fined and jailed with an alacrity that reminded observers of the War Powers Act.

To cope with the growing food shortages, fuel was allocated to farming states according to food produced and population. Those allocations were further implemented on a county by county level by federal authorities who carefully checked vehicular traffic, crops produced, farm equipment on premises, and older records. The paperwork for both farm and industry tripled overnight, but the sporadic breakdowns in energy supply and delivery ceased. All urban dwellers received rationing coupons.

TV specials concentrated on the fact that the economy seemed permanently frozen at a low level, and some of the documentaries seemed decidedly anti-government in stance and rhetoric. Under the licensing procedure authorized by the FCC, stations that agitated for looser controls and more freedom to choose lost their licenses or retained only provisional broadcasting privileges.

By 1992, after a full term in office, the President had fundamentally changed the way the executive branch of the government related to society. Numerous lawsuits challenged the never ending series of executive orders, but the President turned back all attempts at limitation of power at the Supreme Court level. His sheer dominance in style and manner, plus the huge financial support he received from the business community, contributed to his landslide re-election.

During his first term, he removed environmental regulations that hampered business. The ties between business and government became even closer than before. Virtually the entire cabinet came from the Fortune 500. The near-crisis atmosphere engendered by energy shortages, runaway inflation, and economic stagnation was further enhanced by erratic weather throughout the world. All four factors gave impetus to the further centralization of both policymaking and resource allocation. Any last attempt at balancing economic forces between large and small businesses vanished. The government clearly favored big business. Economists ascribed the failure of smaller companies during this time to the changing nature of the world.

The further concentration of capital and production accomplished the oligopolistic desires of the President. He preferred to work with a few concentrated companies rather than whole industries. Only the larger companies could afford the lawyers, lobbyists, and contacts who knew how to navigate in the waters of the federalized economy. Some businesses struggled to survive by putting workers on three-day work weeks, by selling off part of their pension portfolios (at greatly reduced prices), and by borrowing from employees. But rather than the inspiring success stories promised by exponents of economic democracy, the sparse attempts at worker control of businesses were no match for the powerful beneficiaries of centralized planning.

The President and his several new commissions guided the investment decisions of all Americans through punitive taxation, incentives, regulations, and massive purchasing power. Much of the investment financed the larger standing army required to keep the resource-rich nations from internal collapse, or worse yet, internal revolt. Although the increased balance of terror worldwide was hardly conducive to a lasting peace, at least there was no more hypocrisy on the part of Americans. Americans wanted and required key raw materials. As long as the necessary supply channels remained clear, little else mattered.

The expenses of increased bureaucracy and a larger military were borne by the private sector. The combination of eight years of a nongrowth economy and a growing public sector meant that wealth was expropriated from taxpayers. The real net worth of Americans declined almost across the board. The President repeatedly made the case that only through such an extended period of "discipline, organization, and management" could America recoup its power. For most Americans, the "sacrifices" were satisfactory in that they seemed to create a stable and strong government that was at least "doing something."

The President acted swiftly to solve the nation's energy shortages. Together with the Energy Mobilization Board, a Nuclear Management Corps took over the entire nuclear system from beginning to end. The plants were still owned by utilities, but were no longer operated by them. Many hindering regulations were relaxed. Energy bonds financed the extensive development of synthetic fuel plants.

The move toward greater government control in the energy field, as well as the increased military posture, offended many Americans accustomed to protesting government policies with impunity. But the initial draft resistance marches and protests after the invasion of Iran in 1989 were extinguished suddenly, if not brutally, by the National Guard. In his second term, the President became even less tolerant of dissent. All forms of overt protest met force and the near certainty of detention. The American protest movement had never met anything like this response. And there was no public outcry to fall back on. The stories were treated as routine news; none of the anti-draft leaders were lionized in the press. Similar actions quashed the anti-nuclear movement, especially demonstrations that occurred at weapons centers. The institution of the Energy Emergencies Act in 1988 gave the federal government the right to stop demonstrations at any power plant in the name of "national security."

Because management and control were essential to government policy, federal I.D. cards using social security numbers were issued in 1994. The welfare system required the new identity card. All those receiving welfare had to show up at government work centers or forfeit their checks. The welfare corps became a cheap work force that the government used extensively. Although there were vague comparisons to the WPA and Roosevelt, the new corps lacked the esprit and public works consciousness that had characterized the Great Depression. Workers loaded military ships, cleaned up military bases, and worked in detention centers.

In 1995, the National Health Insurance program became

available to anyone who wanted it. But the better medical centers ignored the red tape it required and concentrated on selling their services to those who could afford them. Government-authorized hospitals imposed long waits, long registration processes, and did not always give adequate care.

In the same year, the Secretary of Defense unified the military into one service: U.S. Military Forces, Air, Naval, and Land. Not only did this reduce costs, but effectiveness and spirit were restored. The status of military personnel grew as the Forces pursued a policy of upgrading both staff and prestige. Several successful operations — in the Philippines, Jamaica, and Iran — helped rebuild public confidence and made heroes of officers.

By the year 1996, the economy started to turn up. America was at last doing better than many of its allies, including France, England, and Germany. France, Italy, and the U.K. had become decidedly socialist nations. Northern Europe swung to the right along with West Germany, Switzerland, and Austria. Eastern Europe remained nominally communistic, but worker uprisings and defections from the military were commonplace. The Soviet Union had to put down two internal uprisings in Asia, faced nuclear blackmail by a Soviet missile subcrew, and weathered a continuing series of skirmishes along its entire Asian border from Iran to China. The Soviets' attempt to move into Turkey following the civil war there was thwarted by a secret nuclear device delivered by truck to their key staging area. The small bomb, a product of Iraqi and Pakistani terrorist efforts, destroyed the better part of the Soviet force before it got started.

American military intervention in Mexico kept Marxists out of power there. Most of South America and Africa are still affected by various wars and continuing turmoil. Only Japan, Korea, China, Taiwan, Hong Kong, Malaysia, and Singapore have really prospered. With the leadership of the Japanese, Asia has become the economic center of the world.

In the U.S. a new "elite" emerged. The President called for a new dedicated "corps" of people ready to serve the public interest. These new managers soon became the center of things,

61

like the core of a computer memory. Thus they were known as "Cores." Cores came from MIT, Stanford, IBM, Xerox, SRI, Rand, and the media. They knew how to get things done. They used computers, sophisticated telecommunications, behavior modification, and scientific management.

Presently, Cores are still dedicated and hardworking, and they are rewarded well. What privileges there are they get. They speak a technical language full of terms such as daemons, frobs, TECOs, PDLs, and wizards. Most people see them as the best and brightest finally able to show what they know how to do. The systems analysts in government help set targets (for example, mileage standards for cars) and negotiate them with business. Failure to meet targets does not produce complex litigation. But noncooperative companies may have their tax benefits removed. More and more the management of the giant companies and the government is by the Cores. They all share the same worldview. They have become a kind of secular priesthood. Few are married — they work too hard and long. They often live in shared condominiums. One of their benefits is access to government-owned electric cars. The Cores seem to be drifting further from the general populace into their own private world. There are debates among some learned elements about the ethics of such a technocratic system. But in the end their arguments founder on the pragmatic reality of a technocratic management system that is the least destructive system for achieving growth and economic equilibrium.

If you are the sort of person who keeps a neat bedroom, you might never have noticed the change of moral regime. Only when you step out of line do you discover how narrow and neat a line it is, and how grave are the consequences of falling off it, however inadvertently.

The totally administered society makes most interactions much easier. With the aid of microelectronics, bookkeeping is simple. Most accounting is electronic. Cash is all but unnecessary. Credit is instant, and doesn't demand a pocketful of cumbersome cards. Sensors for the print and pressure of a purchaser's fingers prove infallible. Using your own unique touch signature, you can charge your purchases to an account whose balance is always up to date.

The same touch signature works in toll booths, entrances and exits from locked buildings, everywhere that people used to fumble with keys or cash. Of course, the convenience of the touch system has its drawbacks. The fact that you have to *touch in* to transact business, travel, or enter most buildings means that you leave tracks. Like a new snow on the surface of everyday existence, the network of electronic monitors allows bureaucratic hunters to trace your every move.

Cash was tedious, but at least it was anonymous. Of course, if you stay well within the law, who cares if "they" know where you are at every minute of every day. Getting rid of the keys and the cash and the credit cards allows you to wear pants with no pockets — a much cleaner, trimmer look.

For most people the new order works. Their lives are comfortable and secure. Crime is down. Job security is up. National security is up. Things may not be progressing the way they used to, but they do work. Shortages are a thing of the past. The economy is more efficient and productive. Inflation is only 5 percent. Officially, unemployment is zero. Few young couples can afford a new house, but they are staying home longer anyway in order to contribute to their families' incomes. The family has become, for most Americans, an increasingly important part of life.

For the poor, the outcast, the outlaws, and the rebellious, life is lived on the margins. There are only about 20 million of them. They have their own barter economy. Drugs, those that are still illegal, provide income, along with prostitution and other more serious crimes. Many are people who had protested the increasing regimentation of life. Quickly they become nonpeople, unable to get work or travel once their official identification numbers are cancelled. They cannot make long-distance calls, open bank accounts, or perform other transactions that require an I.D. and a touch. They are not officially punished, just left out.

Many prefer life out on the edge. Life is less tame there. The areas where such people congregate — former slums, some suburbs, some small towns — become untamed. Joy joints, the current version of speakeasys, are common there and all manner of illicit activity can be found in them. To get into a joy joint is to get "kicked back," a phrase coined in Southern California in the seventies. A whole class of people are known as "kicks." If you lack an I.D., you have to be a kick, or so goes the common wisdom.

Occasionally it is reported that some staid, middle-class sort has been caught in an altercation in a joy joint. For a "mass" to get caught in a "J.J." is a tolerable impropriety; it is seen as an adventurous thing to do. But for a Core to get caught is a very serious matter. Their power demands a much higher standard. A Core is usually fired if caught.

A new constitutional amendment, ratified in 1999, to take effect on January 1, 2000, makes a major change. A new integrative branch of government is created. Its function is to evaluate the impact of any major proposed government or business action. A negative evaluation is a veto. It also sets all official projections and performance targets. Its only remedy is fiscal. It may reduce budgets in proportion to the magnitude of failure. Its main reason for being is to insure that the system does not get out of touch with reality again, to keep expectations and means within reach of each, to make sure the system receives proper management.

This scenario addressed the question: What happens to American society when threats to economic growth and national security become too great? Expectations are shaken by a series of external events over which we have no control. What will America do when its oil is reduced by one-third or one-half? Will we gracefully cut back on consumption, or go out and fight for it? Will we become self-reflective, or will we try to recreate the past?

Survival values approach these problems by appealing to central authority. A collective fear of the future manifests itself through rigid controls on speech, politics, and freedom. In a sense we become intolerant of ourselves. A gray condition of repression replaces our acceptance of different ways of life. Heterogeneity seems to be a threat when a troubled world already offers too many confrontations with differences outside our own borders. We vote away our fear and vest power in seemingly competent figures who promise peace, uniformity, and security — perfect antidotes to the anxiety that motivates so many personal choices. Having been taught that individuals are powerless, we abdicate responsibility and seek shelter in authoritarianism when a genuine need for individual action and responsibility arises.

Is it plausible? Is this the stuff Americans are made of? Undoubtedly, most would answer no. Nevertheless, it should be remembered that a relatively small plurality can nominate and elect a President; that recent events on gas lines and the sporadic beatings of Iranians during the hostage crisis demonstrate our intolerance to adversity and powerlessness. History has shown that when a nation experiences failure or lowered self-esteem, it will sometimes turn on itself or others in order to restore its identity.

The desire for authoritarian responses to crises has always been at war with the virtues of smalltown America. There is a long-standing tradition of self-reliance from the Yankees to the cowboys. Perhaps the recent shift of the demographic trend away from big cities toward smaller cities and towns is indicative of a more basic trend. If Americans respond to the demise of the Official Future with frugal values, then the same driving trends that provoked the Center Holds may give rise to Mature Calm instead.

Table 5
Statistics: The Center Holds

	1980	2000
World Population (in millions)	4,500	6,800
U.S. Population (in millions)	226	268
World GNP (in billions)	7,000	16,000
U.S. GNP (in billions)	2,600	3,068
U.S. Per Capita Disposable Income	8,100	8,200
U.S. Per Capita Consumption Expenditures	7,400	7,400
Average World Energy Prices ($/bbl crude)	35	80
Energy Consumption (quads)	78	85
Energy Supply by Source (quads)		
Domestic Oil	20	18
Imported Oil	15	10
Shale Oil	0	2
Natural Gas	20	16
Coal	17	23
Conventional Nuclear	3	8
Nuclear Breeder	0	1
Solar, Hydropower, and Other	3	8
Percentage of Income Spent On		
Housing	21	20
Food	20	23
Clothing	8	5
Medical Care	10	4
Transportation	15	10

Note: 1 quad = 10^{15} Btu/yr; all dollar figures are in 1980 dollars.

Table 6
Trends: The Center Holds

Countries growing economically: *

Japan	Malaysia
Korea	Singapore
Taiwan	Indonesia
China	

Countries contracting economically: **

Pakistan	Spain
Egypt	Poland
Turkey	

Occupations which are rapidly growing in demand:

Programmers	Managers
Media specialists	Lawyers
Behavioral engineers	Druggists
Policy analysts	

Occupations which are shrinking in demand:

Bankers	Musicians
Designers	Teachers
Craftsmen	Clergymen

Businesses which are growing:

Energy	Aerospace
Communications	Pharmaceutics
Electronics	Insurance

Businesses which are contracting:
Publishing

*Top 10 percent in growth of GNP 1995-2000
**Bottom 5 percent in growth of GNP 1995-2000

Chapter V

Mature Calm

In Mature Calm we wake up, jolted to attention by a decade of uncertainty and ineptitude, and decide that it is time to drop ideological barriers. America rediscovers that a nation forms in order to help itself, not to place limitations on citizens in a belief that people cannot be trusted. Just as the Nixon administration opened the doors to the "peril" of China to the delight of the radical left, so do the actions of a series of conservative administrations implement many of the programs once dear to the ecological left. The shift to conservatism allows Americans a breathing space in which they can be less selfish and more prudent, less impulsive and more thoughtful. Renewed American commitments calm a bellicose world and provide two decades of stability and peace. During this time there are no great strides made in any one direction: Russia remains mistrusted, nuclear weapons are stockpiled, environmental problems continue, and economic inequities resist change. Nevertheless, the nation does not feel it is slipping backward. Despite the fact that it is a slower growing economy and that energy is allocated by the high price of the marketplace, America feels safe. The wisdom of senior leaders restores the power of the largest demographic group, those over fifty-five. Young people stay in school, families buy homes, and the Yankees win the World Series. We all wonder what the big scare was about in the late seventies. Did we lack faith in the momentum of the commonplace?

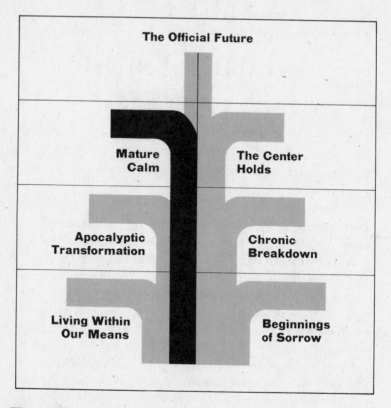

The Official Future

Mature Calm

The Center Holds

Apocalyptic Transformation

Chronic Breakdown

Living Within Our Means

Beginnings of Sorrow

M ANY OF THE TRENDS that had been predicted by sociologists, ecologists, and those who espoused renewable sources of energy came to be accepted as policy by a conservative political establishment during the early eighties. Oil still flowed from the Middle East, but the continued radicalization of successive regimes there foretold a political uncertainty that was not in the best interests of any of the big powers. Faced with the erratic nature of energy supplies, the President and Congress created an energy program both sweeping in its mandate and resolute in its course. Conservation came home as the holy word of conservatives.

When it became obvious that none of the government-backed programs or incentives, for drilling or synfuels or nuclear, would yield any appreciable results during the eighties, a group of supply-side economists working within the administration drafted a report detailing the need for conservation in order that their economic programs work. Without sufficient energy, stimulation of supply in the short term would lead to massive inflation without corresponding production increases of energy, thus cancelling the effectiveness of such policies. In strict economic terms, they showed that "first-order" conservation was less expensive than any other type of energy production possible during the eighties. They therefore recommended vigorous administration support of policies that they had rhetorically discounted while campaigning. The conservation rebate tax quickly passed both houses, one of the most radical pieces of legislation ever passed by a Republican administration, since it was essentially a tax on the rich that had been championed by liberals for years. A $1 tax was levied on all gasoline purchases, then rebated at the end of the year on a per capita basis. Those who used little or no gasoline received money. Those who used more than the per capita average paid money. Those whose gasoline consumption equaled the national average received most or all of their tax money back as a refund at the end of the year. The tax started out at $1 but graduated to $2 by 1985. In order to buoy up the domestic automobile industry, a 7 percent tax credit was granted all American-made automobiles that had a 35 mpg efficiency or better. On the incentive side, investors received a two-for-one write-off for all petroleum and gas exploration, a move that doubled United States drilling and exploration within six years.

Congress and the administration reworked the IRS code and created a new tax structure. Government acted on the philosophy that carrots work better than sticks. In the spirit of free enterprise, those who provided new wealth and resources for the country were amply rewarded by the tax code. Those who wasted and squandered were punished. It was as if the government adopted the notion of behavior modification by putting the nation on a profit-sharing plan. The profits in this case were the savings in resources from consumptive sectors, savings that could be channeled back into productive sectors.

Of course, price had much to do with the new-found conservative spirit. While the rest of the world had become accustomed to high gas prices in previous decades, Middle Eastern instability, coupled with domestic decontrol, created a rise in prices unprecedented in the United States. While domestic consumption of oil fell 6 percent per year for three years, the GNP managed to grow slightly. Eliminated from the system was the fat, not the meat. For all the initial grumbling, the nation seemed happier a few pounds lighter. Getting ahead was harder, so work became more respected. In real terms, family incomes declined. But instead of the criticism once heard by Republicans toward their freely spending opponents, the new conservative politicians talked about sacrifices ahead caused by the foolishness of the past, and somehow it was all palatable.

At the same time, the strange symbiosis between the Right and the Left revived some of the radical movement of the sixties. With fatherly conservatives at the helm once more, local organizations arose to fight for decentralized solutions to problems. It was a curious political fight since it had been the Right that had argued longest for states' rights and local control. Instead, the Right now found itself defending more centralization. Several states instituted stricter controls on energy produced within their boundaries, including taxation and environmental controls that often limited the export of oil and gas across state lines. These efforts were vigorously attacked by the federal government and the Justice Department in particular. California could find the support to build and service an LNG port, but it could not find reason to allow a pipeline out of the state to export the gas. Alaska found new ways to keep its oil with a transport tax that made the oil more attractive to domestic users and suppliers. Like the Saudis, the Alaskans thought it more profitable to export fertilizers and plastics than gas and oil. This burst of states' chauvinism was hardly what the country needed. But by the mid-eighties, New England, for example, was producing much of its housing heat by wood and could thumb its nose at the constant disruption in supplies experienced in bordering states. Protest groups continued to argue against nuclear energy and other polluting, nonrenewable energy sources.

The highly pragmatic nature of an almost corporate Presidency dealt with problems as would any business: benefits, risks, tradeoffs. In the political arena of the eighties, few spoiled for a fight, but fewer still abandoned sincerely held beliefs. The horrors of nuclear waste were so well known and publicized that all plans for breeder reactors were permanently shelved. The broadly articulated tradeoff between environmentalists, the public, the government, and industry was that none of the existing nuclear plants would be shut down. All plants under construction would be properly commissioned. No more would be built, provided that some relaxation in emission standards for coal were allowed. While Westinghouse on the one hand and the American Lung Association and Friends of the Earth on the other cried foul, a reluctant majority proceeded with difficult national issues.

The government took on the role of arbiter of scarce resources. Every year one or more items fell into questionable status in terms of long-term supply, and in most cases, the government carefully formed plans, either through incentives or by stockpiling, to ensure stability. Government-to-government deals between America and other countries secured long-term supplies of mineral resources. The planning eased some of the world tensions caused by the Carter doctrine. Scarce resources were critical to the well-being of the United States, but instead of military force, America found the tradeoffs more effective.

The economy was the talk of the decade. Economic theories sprouted like weeds and financial planners enjoyed a boom. The government concentrated most of its economic efforts in two categories. First, it tried to restore some semblance of balance to the monetary policies of the Federal Reserve. Second, government encouraged the productive sector of the economy, much to the detriment of the service and professional economy.

Productivity was at a premium and industry indices received attention from both the President and the press.

While the public sector grappled with productivity and prices, the private sector struggled with consumption. There was a decade-long shift of consumer patterns toward goods that promised nonobsolescence or at least greater durability. Consumerism added new concerns, including ease of repair, availability of spare parts, and life-of-product costs. The scandal of the eighties was the discovery that U.S. automakers had deliberately designed car engines and working components so that individual owners could not work on their cars, nor could nonfactory-owned or trained shops repair them, since many of the tools required were proprietary. Automakers had made a quiet decision in the early seventies that cars should be like Xerox copiers and Polaroid cameras: beautiful machines until they break down and become mechanical hostages for which their owners must pay to get repair and supplies — in this case, spare parts — from their sole-source manufacturers. After intra-corporate memos leaked the extent of the practice in the industry, a flurry of lawsuits by the government and class-action consumer groups claimed a conspiracy to prevent competition. The imbroglio lasted for years and did nothing to restore luster to U.S. automakers.

In the meantime, a consortium of small parts manufacturers and steelmakers announced in 1986 the formation of a company that would manufacture and market the first new U.S. automobile in over fifty years. Its product name, TRANSIT, symbolized the company's goal of a singular vehicle with few options that could be made and repaired with easily available parts. It was literally a nuts and bolts operation, and the first TRANSIT looked very functional. With a top speed of fifty miles per hour and city mileage of 60 mpg, or 96 kpg, it was a car with the potential for twenty years of useful life. TRANSIT officials said that when existing engines wore out, they expected to have a new engine that could be bolted into the existing frame and that would get 160 kpg. All future innovations could be adapted to all models, ensuring users that their vehicles could constantly evolve as technology changed.

The increasing economic sophistication of the American consumer spilled over into other areas. One of the most confusing issues of the eighties was the problem of government economic indices. As more and more people came to learn and understand their meaning and potential implications, there arose widespread doubts about their actual purpose and accuracy. Many of the statistical methods used by the Commerce Department originated way back in the twenties in a very different economic world. One of the problem statistics in the eighties was unemployment. With millions being added to the work force every year, unemployment nevertheless climbed inexorably. It became obvious to many that much of the expansion of the labor force was discretionary; that is, people were choosing to work who had no need or strong desire to work. As these people went in and out of the labor force, unemployment figures rose. Second, as domestic frugality increased, taxpayers questioned the Consumer Price Index as a measure of inflating government transfer payments. Since consumers had already cut back on meat, fuel, movies, and travel, why should government employees get paid to maintain their old lifestyle with bi-annual wage increases? Third, as consumers shifted to durables and away from throw-away goods, the net effect was a drop in the Gross National Product several years after the original purchase, when the consumer normally would replace an item. The government, at one time greatly agitated about such dips in GNP, now began a forceful argument to defend GNP stabilization. The President's Council of Economic Advisors argued that as the population changed its buying habits, the shift to durables would not necessarily affect the economy adversely because durable products would require higher inputs of skilled labor. While turnover of these items tended to be reduced, the amount of labor in the shrinking market would go up, thereby nullifying the negative effect that might have been expected.

The answer to the argument over indices was the appointment

75

of a Presidential Commission on Commerce. It spent two years studying the way the economy was measured and how those measurements impacted unions, social security recipients, banking, trade, currency issuance, and bonds. Its recommendations produced sweeping changes in most areas, especially in the way citizens perceived relative economic health. Several new indices included the Conservation Index, which recorded the increased efficiency gained by industry in relation to energy consumption and material production. The long-term effect was to give everyone a new way to look at the economy, with an emphasis on such nonmonetary values as self-reliance, nonobsolescence, conservation, and ingenuity — values that were always skirted by the old economic indices.

Many people reacted against the dominance of the culture by economics. Money seemed to be the final measure of everything. Economic jargon crept through the language and suffused conversation on everything from sports to music. It was as if the population were mesmerized by the topic. Others saw the emphasis as hopeful, leading to a better understanding between consumption, resources, and production.

But while economics seemed to rule the decade, at least it hadn't ruined it as had been feared. Americans seemed to thrive in difficult economic times. Instead of crumpling under the pressure, most took the shortages, high prices, and tougher times as a challenging game to be played skillfully.

Many of the changes during these decades happened so slowly that they were not immediately noticeable, for example, the resurgence of the small town and the profound demographic shift accompanying it. College-educated youth from the cities continued their exodus to rural areas. Instead of heading for the woods, many of them set up shop in the village. Just when it seemed that many of the lost skills and arts of our forebears were to be forever lost between the pages of Eric Sloane's books, tens of thousands of young craftspersons and artisans revived long forgotten skills. The hot tub revolution eventually spawned the revival of the cooperage. Blacksmiths became numerous enough for a national convention in 1988. Blacksmiths not only acted as iron-mongers, but many began making tools to order complete with handturned, native wood handles.

The explosion of smalltown culture stimulated a similar increase in live music. With more and more people off in the country, unplugged from TV or just disinterested, there was a resurgence in smalltime country, jug, and bluegrass bands; folk singers, minstrels, and traveling road shows. Networks of smalltown entertainment circuits spread a festive and heel-kicking air that had been lost for decades. Just as the folk-rock music of the sixties had resulted in an explosion in the record industry, this new form of music had its correlative commercial wave. But instead of CBS and Warner, the new labels read Beanville, Red's Neck, and many more — a profusion of smalltime record companies. Instead of acting as producers, the major record companies functioned as distributors of those labels they thought had national or regional appeal.

Another demonstration of smalltownism was demographic. While city schools continued to close one by one for lack of enrollments, country schools burst at the seams. At first the shift was not recognized by state and federal agencies as they acted on the continued assumption that cities should get the bulk of federal aid. The faltering cities received large infusions of capital and ended up buying off the poor. The pall of urban bureaucratic charity contrasted with the vitality of small towns where the poor were having a better time on less money.

The move toward small towns was not just a romantic fixation. During the eighties, it was still popularly assumed that living country-style was part of the post-industrial reaction to complexity and technology, and that those who left the urban areas were slightly nostalgic if not Luddite. When the 1990 Census showed how dramatic the shift had become, it became clearer that the migration was in fact a reversal of the economic considerations that had driven families off the land in the first place. The cities no longer offered the best jobs, the most security, or the richest lifestyle. They had become so burdened by scale and infrastructural costs that they could no longer support their populations with services and security. Police were beefed up, but streets were dirtier. Teachers were better paid, but the schools were dangerous. Housing was available, but rents were expensive. Food was costly, tension unbearable, and smog unabated.

As the migration to rural America proceeded, it took with it many small businesses — manufacturing, service, and communication. Many people left with their employers en masse to find a better environment. Electronics companies continued to be the growth industry they were in the eighties, and their technology allowed them the privilege of remoteness since they relied little upon steel, trucking, railroads, and freeways. When a small, high-tech company moved to a small town, a ripple effect typically produced a new food store, bookstore, and bakery, as well as a bicycle shop, graphics and design studio, printing press, community garden project, a babysitting co-op, a musical society, and a new surge of community activity in local schools. Each migration and settlement had its tensions, problems, and transitional crises, but there was no question that the hybridization of country folk with city folk in small towns and villages produced a vital living environment that was very attractive. Instead of pouring money into the cities, many people hedged their urban bets by putting money into their own favorite town and looked forward to the time they would move to it.

Many who attempted the transition failed. Some could not adapt to lower wages or to the more modest lifestyle. Others missed the tension they had once dreaded. Others simply did not get along, refused to learn the lesson of smalltown diplomacy, and soon found themselves none too subtly ostracized for untoward remarks and actions. Long hair was never a problem in these resettlement activities, but big mouths were.

One of the major benefits of country living was the cost of food. Following the eruption of Mt. St. Helens, agricultural production in the United States became more erratic. The seventh eruption in 1987 coincided with (most say caused) the coldest summer in

California history and unseasonal rains throughout the year. While keeping the hills green, the rain ruined many of the fruit and vegetable crops and cost farmers dearly. Instead of being a one-year problem, Mt. St. Helens continued to erupt, as did two more peaks in the Cascades. Ash and steam poured out for more than a decade. Not only were the areas directly in the path of the fallout affected, but all of the Midwest slowly fell under the effects of the ash. By 1990, the temperature of the earth had dropped nearly two degrees. Canada was forced to curtail its wheat exports; and twice during the decade, it held wheat back for reserves. Prices of food climbed. When Mt. Hood erupted in 1991, it was obvious that the problem was not going to go away for the next decade, possibly not for many decades. The increased activity was by then making substantial changes in the weather and hopes that the disruptions were temporary were abandoned. While those who lived in the country also suffered high food costs, most were producers too. As hot-weather crops such as tomatoes and corn began to fail in traditional growing areas, farmers and gardeners found better luck with potatoes, cabbage, berries, and other plants that thrived in the considerably cooler weather.

City populations bore the brunt of the climatic shift. Not all of the price increases were supply oriented. Petty thoughts of larceny possessed produce dealers as it became obvious that supply had gained mastery over the fickle demand of the marketplace. People cut back on fresh produce temporarily, but eventually returned since no price refuge could be found in frozen or canned foods either. All staples increased and shortages were common, but the news of the food "crisis" was worse than the reality. A shrinking dollar got washed again, this time by food. There was little that government or citizens could do about it as long as the Cascades blew ash over much of America.

Rural areas benefited as farmers' markets thrived and spread. City people learned to buy directly from the open-air markets set up in squares and parking lots. High prices, and the fact that urbanites would stock up heavily on produce in order to save, made the trip to the city worthwhile for the small farmer. Like Beijing, Marseilles, and Dar es Salaam, American cities were invaded in the predawn hours by small trucks laden with food that went directly to customers rather than to stores. With the food also went marijuana that customers could ask for under code names. When someone paid $20 for a bag of string beans, something else was on the bottom of the bag.

The shift in food consumption and purchasing also resulted in other wares being sold on weekends by country craftspersons. With transportation costs soaring, many items that were manufactured and distributed nationally had become more expensive than similar (and better) items that were made locally. Simple tables and chairs far surpassed in quality and price what you could get in furniture stores. Same for clothing, woolens, small casks of wine, and leather shoes. With the merchants came a hodge-podge of jugglers, tarot readers, tatooists, and herbalists. And pickpockets. Whatever the mix, a profound reversal of economic flow was occurring. Country people were doing better than their city cousins, and the lesson, plain for all to read, accelerated the migratory rush, raising the price of country land and depressing urban property all at once.

In the suburbs the change was not as dramatic. While the suburbs experienced some of the plight of the cities — higher transportation and food costs, rising crime and unemployment — they also had some of the advantages of the rural areas in that people had backyards, garages, and, in some cases, small workshops where they could produce for many of their own and their neighbors' needs. The more affluent suburbs seemed to hang onto their image of how things ought to be. Their voters refused to allow small businesses to operate from homes, or food to be grown on school lawns. Otherwise suburbs made whatever adaptive measures were necessary and prudent. People did sewing, tailoring, and sharpening in their homes. Many front lawns became gardens, and food was prominent at flea markets.

By the mid-nineties, a three-tiered society was easily divisible by geography. While the government concentrated on industry, production, and resource allocation, the cities saw their condition deteriorate with little taxpayer sympathy from either Washington or the states. Suburbs that had access to viable industries saw a modest decline in living standards and a tremendous increase in community participation in government, policing, services, and planning. The rural areas that offered good living conditions in terms of food, liberal building codes, friendly people, and ample resources, saw their stock soar. Rural America became the queen of the nineties.

The rest of the world did not fare so well. America was constantly faced with what appeared to be a Hobson's choice: either it forcibly obtained access to resources through military or economic threats, or it had to back down and appear as a declining power. In several instances, the media began a warmongering attitude that inflamed nationalistic passions. While the crises seemed to come relentlessly, the United States government continued to face each separately, not allowing itself to be drawn into the debate between prestige and powerlessness. In Washington the consensus favored a steady hand and a firm resolve. Forswearing gunboat diplomacy, U.S. foreign policy recognized that any type of limited engagement with aligned or nonaligned countries would only worsen its prospects further down the road. The rise of nationalism was accepted as an inevitability. Rather than rising to answer the chest-thumping howls of radical regimes who claimed to have kicked out America, the U.S. merely waited until they needed to restore their economies. The marketplace became a bigger stick. The triumph of American foreign policy lay in recognizing economic power sooner than its scattered enemies did. By the end of the century more countries were basically anti-American, but in terms of overall foreign trade America was still the world's dominant buyer and seller.

In 1999 America was abuzz about the millennium. New photovoltaic technologies have freed the house from dependence on fossil fuels. Automobile usage has shifted heavily toward bicycles, buses, walking, trains, and transits. The health of the nation has improved for the first time since the turn of the century in terms of a decline in degenerative diseases. The problems of toxicity and nuclear waste have both been technologically solved although not fully executed. Mineral recovery techniques have turned old landfill dumps into mines. Genetic engineering did not escape from the bottle to ruin anything; chemical firms that experimented early derived half of their pretax earnings from this technology.

The birthrate is rising slowly, immigration is allowed, and many anti-growth areas now welcome new residents. New York is not fun city, but retains its crown as cultural and financial king. Most of the volcanic disturbances in the West have ceased and the weather is apparently improving. Sixty-three-year-old Colonel Khaddhafi has announced that Libya has perfected a hydrogen bomb. President Carter now lies buried at Plains, Georgia, after a state funeral along Pennsylvania Avenue. Senator John Kennedy watched and saluted not far from where he had watched his father's coffin pass in 1963. The first manned flight to Mars, scheduled to arrive in the year 2002 on the Sea of Storms, leaves Earth later this year. America is leaner and wiser, and any fear that we would perish lies long forgotten as we enter the new century.

In Mature Calm, the United States succeeds on the whole in organizing and using human and material resources to address critical social, economic, and political problems. Overall there is real economic growth. Although the promises of plenty have been well tempered by events, the success of industrial capitalism is sufficient to nudge the aspirations of most along the path of continued hard work and consumption. Because a widely distributed infrastructure of persons, organizations, and groups develop diverse solutions to social, technical, and resource problems, we are not left without options. In Mature Calm, the citizenry is not afraid to adapt, to make choices that will profoundly affect the future — moving, change of livelihood, change of social status. Our problems lead us to recognize regional and personal differences rather than make us yearn for sameness. Our "maturity" is our ability to look beyond symptoms to see syndromes. Systematic change replaces band-aid solutions. Our "calmness" lies in our refusal to get panicked or fear-ridden while we are adjusting to unexpected circumstances. The result is a highly mixed and diverse society with just as many problems as we have today. The critical difference between Mature Calm and the Center Holds stems from different responses to the dislocations of the two decades: in Mature Calm we learn, where we merely react in the Center Holds.

Both the Center Holds and Mature Calm assumed that though our problems might be severe, they could be tolerably addressed by either centralized management to the exclusion of diversity, or by self-reliance coupled with lower expectations. But the problems of the next decades may not be manageable by either central administration or more decentralized solutions. Perhaps the economic misfortunes of Chrysler and New York City are more typical than exceptional. It may mean something that no President has served two full terms in the last two decades, and that average income has not risen in the last decade. The next two scenarios cope with a constellation of driving trends that reflect less favorable conditions than those in the previous two scenarios.

Table 7
Statistics: Mature Calm

	1980	2000
World Population (in millions)	4,500	6,350
U.S. Population (in millions)	226	268
World GNP (in billions)	7,000	16,000
U.S. GNP (in billions)	2,600	4,396
U.S. Per Capita Disposable Income	8,100	10,700
U.S. Per Capita Consumption Expenditures	7,400	8,800
Average World Energy Prices ($/bbl crude)	35	60
Energy Consumption (quads)	78	100
Energy Supply by Source (quads)		
Domestic Oil	20	22
Imported Oil	15	12
Shale Oil	0	2
Natural Gas	20	19
Coal	17	25
Conventional Nuclear	3	9
Nuclear Breeder	0	1
Solar, Hydropower, and Other	3	10
Percentage of Income Spent On		
Housing	21	18
Food	21	23
Clothing	8	7
Medical Care	10	9
Transportation	15	13

Note: 1 quad = 10^{15} Btu/yr; all dollar figures are in 1980 dollars.

Table 8
Trends: Mature Calm

Countries growing economically: *

Japan	Korea
Germany	Brazil
United States	South Africa
France	Australia
Mexico	Israel

Countries contracting economically: **

Vietnam	Ethiopia
Cuba	Sudan
Syria	India
Hungary	

Occupations which are rapidly growing in demand:

Engineers	Musicians
Farmers	Printers
Financial analysts	Professional military officers
Entrepreneurs	Pilots
Small businessmen	Bioengineers
Recyclers	Carpenters

Occupations which are shrinking in demand:

Bureaucrats	Medical administrators
Lawyers	Retail clerks

Businesses which are growing:

Energy (all forms)	Communication
Housing	Education
Financial services	Farming
Information utilities	

*Top 10 percent in growth of GNP 1995-2000
**Bottom 5 percent in growth of GNP 1995-2000

Chapter VI

Chronic Breakdown

Chronic Breakdown is about creeping decay. Anyone who has suffered a week when everything went wrong knows something of what Chronic Breakdown might be like; stretch that week to twenty years, imagine the sufferings of a nation in place of the sufferings of an individual, and you have some sense of this uphill struggle against entropy. The United States finds itself beset on every front by forces it no longer controls. Its destiny seems hopelessly lost. Events seem chaotic and decisions almost futile in the face of randomly negative news. Chronic Breakdown is the future that defies rational planning. Mere coping is the most we can manage.

The events we have chosen to illustrate such a breakdown are not as significant as the mood of pervasive pessimism that characterizes this scenario. The rhythm of decay is an adagio of despair without the percussion of decisive turning points. Progress melts as the main driving trends all worsen. Energy becomes chronically short. Unbalanced economic policies catch up and wreak vengeance on Mr. and Mrs. Homeowner. Like a tired old lion claiming territory it is unable to defend, America watches as smaller, younger countries eat away at its former sphere of influence. It is a sad and dreary sight. The weather is terrible: cold in winter, dry in summer, windy and tempestuous in spring and fall. In many ways Chronic Breakdown is a depression from which no one sees a way out.

A society that functions subnormally becomes accepted as the new reality. People's disillusionment is proportional only to the extent of their realization that what goes down does not always come up. Crises provoke no sense of opportunity, only an ever deeper sense of danger. What little economic activity persists has the air of a scramble for better deck chairs on a doomed Titanic. But America never sinks. We just sail on into the fog, no haven in sight.

In the sixties, E. M. Cioran observed, "You cannot treat destiny." The best you can do in bad times is "to keep abreast of the incurable." In the seventies, Jim Hougan added, in a book entitled Decadence, *"Nero correctly understood that beauty, music and irony can co-exist with disintegration, that the inevitable can be accompanied on the violin." Throughout the eighties and nineties, the slow decline — not the fall — of industrial culture was accompanied by electric guitars and the sound of breaking glass.*

T HE EIGHTIES STARTED with the same business-as-usual attitude that had characterized the preceding decade. That is, nothing was quite consistent with expectations, but we didn't lose our shirts or our country either. The first several years were good, prosperous — even hopeful. Defense spending cushioned the country from any real recessionary influences. Although consumer goods retrenched in reaction to the spending spree that had characterized the late seventies, electronics, aerospace, and energy companies boomed and grew, and took up the slack in employment from the declining consumer goods industry.

The lulling effect of a country satisfied with itself and its achievements left us ill-prepared for what happened then. In retrospect, it should have been obvious that both prosperity and peace were being purchased at the expense of greater stress upon the system. With hindsight we see that there were signs. The rise of white collar crime, increased payoffs, the wildly volatile stock market, and the extraordinary rise in commodities prices should have been seen for what they were: people and institutions struggling to cope with a rapidly deteriorating economy. There

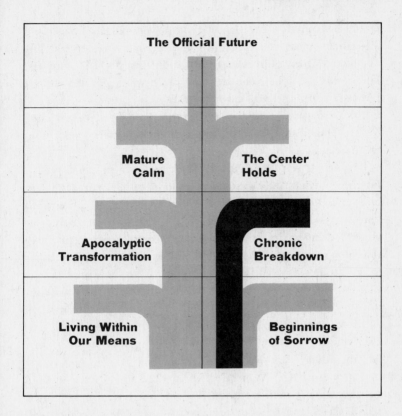

The Official Future

Mature Calm

The Center Holds

Apocalyptic Transformation

Chronic Breakdown

Living Within Our Means

Beginnings of Sorrow

was an actual negative savings rate in 1983 as people borrowed against inflating assets in order to maintain their standards of living. Everyone knew that inflation was here to stay and that the only sensible course was to buy ahead, so no one saved. The country experienced a scrambling, hustling hyperactivity. Individuals and institutions struggled to offset the effects of inflation in a growing economy.

While most facets of the economy grew and prospered, energy supplies became more and more critical. During the winter of 1983, allocated fuel oil almost ran out. Diesel car owners had to park their cars or pump oil from their home heating tanks. Even coal was short due to the rail car deficit. The American response was to pay more and pump more. Reserves were tapped. Rising prices prompted water flooding of played-out oil fields, and legislation sponsored another pipeline parallel to the Alyeska line in Alaska. Mideast forces were bolstered to insure OPEC supplies, but we were caught completely off guard when in 1983 Kuwait fell to a coup and was taken over by the regime of Abdul al Ben-Rashad, who immediately became a popular voice for much of the underlying resentment in Oman, Saudi Arabia, and other OPEC countries.

In a widely televised Barbara Walters interview taped on the fantail of Ben-Rashad's yacht, he announced a 50 percent cut in oil production and called upon his neighbors to follow. His reasoning was simple and effective: the Arabs were selling their oil to feed and maintain a greedy and wasteful Western economy that was paying the Arabs in money that was losing value faster than it could be negotiated. Furthermore, the influx of money was more than these smaller countries could absorb without massive internal disruption. The solution to both problems was to cut production. The West would be forced to conserve and the East could cool its economic heels and consolidate its gains, "Allah willing," Ben-Rashad concluded.

At the April OPEC meeting in London, both Nigerians and Saudi Arabians cautioned Ben-Rashad that such a move might cripple the Western nations permanently. But Ben-Rashad, who had been educated at Yale, pointed out that Lovins, Yergin, and others had shown conclusively that the United States could reduce its energy consumption by 40 percent without a serious drop in its standard of living, and they counterproposed an allocation system based on internal conservation measures rather than wealth alone.

As the meeting dragged on without resolution, the United States dropped hints that such drastic cuts would be seen as a direct threat to its internal security and might have to be dealt with by force. The international outcry that followed ridiculed the U.S. position. Since Ben-Rashad was clearly anti-communist, State Department hints of Russian intervention seemed hollow. Russia said it would view any American intervention in the

Middle East as a serious breach of regional security to be met with direct force. Fearing Soviet incursions into Iran and Saudi Arabia, the U.S. wavered and backed down from its third confrontation in the five years following the Afghanistan invasion and the Turkish "revolution." The prevailing view in Washington was that half of the oil from "free" oil-exporting nations was better than a war that would be hard to win without nuclear weapons, and that might result in no oil from anyone. By that time, everyone knew that Saudi oil fields had been depth mined with nuclear contaminants by English technicians, and the risk of losing all the oil fields stalemated both powers. Ben-Rashad's views finally won over OPEC members, and beginning in 1984, an eighteen-month, phased reduction of oil began throughout the Middle East. Venezuela, Nigeria, and Indonesia abstained from reducing output, but the result was the same — a worldwide shortage.

After an initial panic in the world stock markets and exchanges, cooler heads prevailed. The United States, frustrated and anxious, boldly announced a crash energy program that would bring energy levels back to pre-1984 levels within ten years. When the presidential blue-ribbon commission revealed the plan, scientists and energy experts alike deemed it close to a hoax. Other nations began making their energy plans independent of American policy.

Internationally, oil sold on the spot market for $130 a barrel. Gas was $6 a gallon and rationing took effect. The white market coupons were based on cars owned, a criterion that led to the disappearance of used cars. Many families became three- and four-car families. As long as the cars were parked at home, ran, and remained registered (and insured in some states), the extra coupons were available. This practice finally stopped when the coupons were tied to the number of licensed drivers over eighteen years per car. Nevertheless, abuses were widespread as the nation struggled to change its habits. By 1987, the commute problem solved itself through the unemployment that followed the disastrous Christmas of '86. Until Christmas, Americans had kept calm and positive in the face of international pressure. But that Christmas, sales actually dropped 15 percent from November's sales, which in turn had been 15 percent lower than October's. The consumer goods industries began massive layoffs, as did the steel, auto, rubber, chemical, and machine tool industries. Corporate spending was slashed, first-class sections were eliminated in most planes, and failing restaurants cut prices in hopes of luring back customers. And then disaster struck.

The winter of 1987 was unusually harsh. Oil stocks were exceptionally low because the U.S. had sold a large quantity of reserves to France in an attempt to support that country's partially successful grab of the Libyan oil fields. A few miles west of Seward, Nebraska, train number 4006 was crawling through a blizzard — the seventeenth coal train of the day, a unit train, over a mile long, hundreds of coal cars, carrying thousands of tons of coal to the industrial Midwest. Each day forty-five unit trains ran through Seward, Nebraska. The gap between them was often only minutes. It was like a continuous moving conveyor belt of rail cars. Ahead of the train a signal, heavily laden with snow, was hit by gale force winds for the thirtieth time in an hour. It buckled and folded itself across the tracks in front of the train. Train 4006 could not stop in time and began to peel from the tracks as the engine crossed the crumpled signal. The first forty cars behind the engine left the tracks one by one, chewing up nearly a quarter mile of track in the process. It was a week before that line carried coal again.

A few miles further north and west of the place where train 4006 was shutting down coal trains, nature was preparing an even more bizarre event. A school bus carrying the Grand Island High School basketball team home from a game was crossing a narrow, windswept bridge over the north fork of the Platte River. A gasoline tanker truck just ahead of the bus slid and jackknifed on the icy pavement. The driver swerved to avoid the truck and did manage to miss it, but the slide that followed led to a worse fate. The bus broke through the railing and seemed as if it were headed into the icy river beneath, but its fall was stopped only a dozen feet beneath the roadway. It had rammed into a coal slurry pipeline that ran beneath the bridge. The three-foot-wide pipeline carried powdered coal and water from the great coal fields of the high plains states, Wyoming and Montana, to the synthetic fuel plants and power plants of the Midwest. The bus cracked the pipeline, and a small seam of black fluid was visible around the crack. But the pipeline held, and the bus's fall was checked. However, the rescue efforts to haul the bus off its precipitous ledge finally broke the pipeline. A fountain of black fluid began to pour down onto the icy river beneath. The flow was quickly staunched at its source, but the coal slurry in the pipeline began to freeze in the subzero winds and weather of the blizzard. Within hours, the slurry was slush, and, before the flow could be restored, the pipeline was frozen solid. It took weeks to bring it back up to fluid temperature. The coal supply of St. Louis was stopped dead in the blizzard wastes of central Nebraska.

Ordinarily, this wreck would have only been a minor disaster, but in thin times even a temporary blockage becomes a major disaster. Within seventy-two hours, St. Louis began to freeze. An emergency was declared. All industrial activity ceased. All unnecessary heating and lighting were turned off. All unnecessary appliance use was banned, but supplies began to dwindle rapidly. Within hours of the emergency declaration in St. Louis, the National Guard began a nationwide relief effort to speed supplies to the city. However, the Guard lacked an emergency plan for such a contingency, and the relief effort quickly bogged down in chaos. Some areas that had no reserves were quickly depleted, and they, too, began to freeze. In the widening whirlpool of chaos and crisis, over seven hundred people died and $2 billion were lost.

The crippling domino effect of the winter of '87 dealt a severe blow to the U.S. economy, particularly in the industrial sectors. Energy was chronically short for many years after the incident and the vulnerability of the economy to disruptions of energy supplies became achingly clear. Reduced energy supplies reduced the availability of resources and seriously cut productive capacity at factories. For those workers who managed to keep paying jobs, or the bureaucrats who had seniority, life did not change all that much. But for most Americans, it felt as though the rug had been pulled from beneath their economic feet. Even a three-month layoff could bankrupt a family and leave it with a foreclosed home and a repossessed car. Family relations were strained to the utmost when formerly employed mothers and fathers sat around home with their recently laid-off teenagers. Many women were the first to go since they were employed in service industries. Great antipathy arose toward Hispanic workers still willing to work for $5 an hour. Marriages broke up, and bitterly contested divorces picked over rapidly declining assets.

The one commodity that did not rise with inflation was real estate. Real estate values fell rapidly and took with them speculators, savings and loans, insurance companies, mortgage companies, and most holders of second and third mortgages. The most tragic victims of the falling real estate prices were young homeowners who had bought their homes in the late seventies with low down payments and low mortgage rates of 12 percent and 13 percent. Many had seen their homes double and triple in value in the succeeding years, and had borrowed heavily against their equity in order to finance second homes, vacations, and stock market purchases. Caught up in the rising tide of inflationary pressures, many thought they could make more money in other speculative activities than they were paying out in loan interest, since the 25 percent interest rates were about the same as inflation. Many had serviced negative cash flows by additional borrowing from credit cards, credit unions, and relatives. The mountain of debt was impossible for the large number of unemployed to deal with, and soon "For Sale" and "For Rent" signs dotted neighborhoods as they never had before. A moderately priced, three-bedroom home that had been selling for $300,000 could be had for $100,000, or even less if the buyer had cash.

As per capita income declined and, along with it, a respect for the institutions of the culture, there grew between the crumbling cracks in the old order a new class of beggars and thieves. They were neither the spare change cadgers of earlier decades, nor the trained and practiced thieves that have preyed on almost all societies. Instead, they were bands of raggle-taggle dropouts who demanded more than traditional beggars and less than traditional thieves.

Like the hunters and gatherers who roamed the earth ten thousand years ago, these new tribes tended to be nomadic, or, more accurately, migratory. Chivalry and loyalty were high on the list of the virtues that held these bands together. Unlike the motorcycle gangs that had made only loyalty a large part of their lives while subjecting their "Beetles" to the most sexist of attitudes, these new tribes did a turn on feminism that no one had anticipated. The fairest of the tribe were virtually deified. These priestesses or princesses — both titles were used — became the center of tiny nomadic kingdoms in which there were knights, squires, scribes, and knaves. As ludicrous and anachronistic as the terminology seemed to outsiders, the reality of their lives was far from Arthurian legends. Most of the gangs were convulsively violent and terrified what remained of the gentry. They existed by stealth, expropriation, threats, and force. They avoided the less decadent midland states where they would be more conspicuous. They usually traveled in large, rundown vans or flat-bed pickups, but some traveled by foot and even by horse. Though they satisfied for a time the country's desire for a new mythology, complete with romance, banditry, and adventure, eventually they were driven even further underground.

Since the gangs were known for their violence, the police were understandably reluctant to search them out, especially since their crimes were small by comparison with those of professional criminals. Their demise was finally inflicted by their victims, the citizenry. Because they traveled in small bands, they were subject to violence in turn, and by the middle nineties, vigilante groups found complete justification in attacking them. Once the balance of fear turned, all of the gangs became vulnerable as they traveled through the countryside. Within two years, the savagery of the violence had shifted to the vigilante groups as gang after gang was simply wiped out.

In its 1990 year-end issue, *Newsweek* wrapped up a rough twelve months with a cover story titled "American Guerillas and the Suffering Citizen." The colorful Sadie Grimes, one of the last of the priestesses, shared the cover with an unknown citizen billed as the unknown soldier in the domestic struggle against fear and anarchy. Sadie's story was mostly a summary of earlier reports of daring and romantic exploits, like her fling with the upper New York State police chief whom she seduced in order to get out of jail. Her foil Byron Mitchell's tale was less exciting, but it succeeded in symbolizing the plight of millions who bore the brunt of an outlaw economy:

It was a pothole that finally did it. I was on my way home from work. I was driving my old '74 Ford. I was taking a shortcut when I hit this hole that just swallowed my right front wheel. The shocks were bad. I'd been trying to get new ones for weeks but not a single parts dealer in New Haven could get any shocks from the distributors. "Next week," they kept saying.

So the front tire flatted. There I was on a back street in a rundown neighborhood. The light was fading. I was just setting up the jack when I heard voices behind me. I could feel the fear in the back of my neck. They surrounded me, three of the gypsies. Without a word one of them simply pulled the jack handle out of the jack — my own jack handle — and held it out toward my hip pocket. I took out my wallet and opened it. He took out just the cash, turned, and the three of them walked away. After two or three steps the one with the jack handle turned and threw it through my front windshield. It took me five months to get another windshield.

Those kids knew I was scared. They knew what I had been seeing on the news, the killings and the beatings. They knew I was getting off easy. I could see it in their eyes. It was almost as if they had to smash the windshield just because I was getting off too easy.

And I knew I was getting off easy. I only had about twenty new dollars on me, and two or three hundred of the old. They might have wanted the car.

By 1989, a serious problem had arisen from the inflation/ unemployment cycle. U.S. government revenues began to shrink. Since income taxes had been frozen in 1984 by the Anderson-Baker Act to a fixed percentage of income with increases indexed to consumer prices, there was no way that increased taxes could be levied without a constitutional amendment. By 1990, the gap between government spending and income was so large that reports began to be circulated that the U.S. government was going to default on its obligations. When Secretary of the Treasury Kohler announced in March of that year that further repayments of principal on U.S. securities would be temporarily suspended until a "complete review" of the alternatives available to the Treasury could be established and evaluated, the bond market collapsed in a heap.

While the nation reeled from the impact of worthless savings bonds, shattered pensions, and the default of the social security system, the Treasury announced in April its solution: the "new dollar," available within three weeks at all commercial and Federal Reserve Banks, for twenty "old dollars." The government admitted what gold bugs and speculators had been saying for years — the dollar had very little value. All bonds and government obligations would, from that day, be redeemable in new dollars at the 20:1 ratio. Social security would resume in new dollars with no index to the CPI. The Treasury, which had been quietly buying gold for the past year, also announced that the new dollar would be backed by gold at the rate of one hundred new dollars per ounce.

The devaluation of U.S. currency dealt another blow to an already reeling economy. By 1990, the GNP had declined 26 percent from the high in 1985. Corporations took the devaluation as an opportunity to "adjust" prices, but many items were not reduced to 1/20th as was expected. The massive losses suffered by multinationals on their foreign exchanges during that year created new debt and, in some cases, bankruptcies. Many had to raise prices simply to service their debt and recover their capital base. Expansion was further cut by the loss of confidence, and more jobs were lost in the capital goods sector.

The devaluation let loose waves of indignation and recriminations against the government. Bureaucratic workers felt the hostility of the general populace. Whereas wage earners were suffering from the impact of repeated economic downturns, government employees were protected by cost-of-living increases and seniority clauses. While unemployment hovered around 26 percent in 1990, the government work force had declined by only 2 percent since 1982. Many had called for a massive government reduction in order to cure fiscal insolvency. Instead, the government changed the currency. People were infuriated. What had long simmered as a suspicion that the government really didn't care at all for the citizenry seemed utterly confirmed, and major social schisms resulted. Government buildings were vandalized and equipment was stolen. Postal workers were harassed while making their rounds. The government became a scapegoat, particularly since people now "knew" that there would be no return to the easy ways of the seventies. Life was hard and getting harder, and many people took the attitude that it should therefore be hard for everyone. Government inspectors were hustled out of meat plants and factories at the barrel of a union shotgun. Government regulation of industry had to be carried out by the militia if it was to be enforced at all.

America's strength became its weakness. Our pluralism, our defense of individual liberty, made us a nation of leaders with no followers. Leaders acquired a habit of jumping on their high horses and riding off in all directions at once. No coherent vision guided the many solutions attempted for the social problems of the nineties. Everyone seemed to have the answer, but no one heard the same question. The confusion of ideologies and pseudo-religions was ominous.

By 1995, the number of registered, tax-exempt church orders bulged to well above fifty thousand — up over 50 percent from just a decade earlier when cults were already flourishing. At the same time, the number of political parties was burgeoning. The Democrats and the Republicans were still number one and number two, but the Libertarians, the Black Separatists, the Alliance, and the Communalists were all making bids strong enough to carry the country's legislature toward a model that was increasingly French.

Meanwhile large corporations, particularly the multinationals, waged an increasingly strong campaign for what would be, in effect, the elimination of politics. They had gained a number of persuasive intellectual apologists for their position that a free market was the best system for the administration of those social services "the so-called public sector" perpetually bungled. Ironically they argued for what Marx called *the withering away of the state*. National boundaries had become increasingly anachronistic in the world marketplace.

This great variety of visions made action in concert a virtual impossibility. Consequently, America, the great power, became impotent. "Power," according to political philosopher Hannah Arendt, "corresponds to the human ability not just to act but to act in concert. Power is never the property of an individual; it belongs to a group and remains in existence only so long as the group keeps together." As America came apart through the slow process of chronic breakdown, its power did not shift into the hands of any one group. It simply ebbed as if through a sieve that emptied directly into the earth.

Squabbling and fighting between the Democratic and Republican parties soon vanished as both saw the threat to their dominance posed by other parties. Both political parties had become heavily dependent on business contributions for support. Though the traditional business money still flowed to Republicans, Democrats were getting elected; big business contributed to Democrats in order to retain access to legislators. In any case, both major parties had become indistinguishable and both represented the industrial infrastructure. The repeated economic shocks of the late eighties and early nineties had stopped any type of industrial expansion or innovation. Very few new companies were starting up, while many smaller and medium-sized companies either went out of business or were bought out of business, usually at a discount from their true value. As large de facto cartels formed in industry and resources, the consolidation of economic muscle flowed directly to both parties.

When anti-government riots reached epidemic proportions, a "bi-partisan" presidential task force recommended that the National Guard train special urban units that would work with the FBI to stop domestic violence. The new para-military security force, dubbed the "Urban Dogs," was hated by the lower classes (which by now included much of the middle classes) and welcomed by those who still saw their fortunes and livelihoods intact. Large corporations, seen as particularly close to these policies, companies such as ITT, Con Edison, and McDermott, asked for and received special protection from the Urban Guard. While occasional riots broke out near large corporate and government buildings, leaders urged the citizenry to put shoulders to the wheel and set America right again. There was not the slightest indication from national leaders that any widespread questioning of the assumptions governing economic and social policies would change things. The old political party lines sounded archaic, but there was little save violence and decadence to answer it, hardly an answer at all. In the 1994 State of the Union address, President William Milbergs declared: ". . . before us lie two very different worlds. The choices that inform our lives and ultimately government policy are the choices of civilization or corruption, a lasting peace or chaotic violence. The republic has been tested again and again by those who would see the great American destiny destroyed and replaced by the forces of totalitarianism. We stand tonight in witness of all that we hold sacred. I stand in front of you, the people, to declare irrevocably, that the United States of America has not, is not, and shall not give in to any persons, groups, or organizations that would oppose and undermine the dream of democracy. We are one of the last free nations left upon the earth. As President of this nation, let my voice be heard clearly above the din of anarchy: I pledge allegiance to the United States of America, to one nation under God, with liberty. . . ."

The speech went on to say that the United States was prepared to wage an all-out attack against any and all groups who actively worked against the interests of government.

As violence subsided, or was suppressed, a quieter decadence ran rampant. As has happened in other declining cultures, a sense of alienation gave aid and inspiration to the arts. A cabaret culture sprang up from the mulch and detritus of decaying institutions. Every attempt to resuscitate the old order became the butt of humor. Every earnest reformer was made to play straight man for the new satirists. It seemed as though the American people were incapable of taking anything seriously, salvation and damnation included.

The fashion of decadence was not restricted to a catalogue of drugs, crimes, and petty vandalism. The art of the put-on extended into the highest reaches of public and private enterprise. In 1992, Tex Waters exploited his popularity as a recording star to run for office in the presidential elections. His write-in campaign, sponsored solely by three songs that successively reached the top forty, netted fully 9 percent of the ballots cast.

While some analysts argued that his spoiler put-on had swung the election for the Republicans by taking votes away from the Democratic candidate, most agreed that Waters's candidacy had been largely responsible for the turnaround in the steady decline of voter participation. His 9 percent of the vote represented voters who would not have come to the polls had it not been for his high decibel exhortations. He roared in one of his songs, "The trouble with elections is that government always wins," and Waters claimed to offer an alternative to any government whatever. His anarchistic lyrics did not attract Democrats as much as the totally disaffected, who came forth in droves to boost participation from 34 percent of the eligible electorate in 1988 to 38 percent in

1992 — the first increase after decades of steadily declining voter participation.

People's inability to look ahead with hope had the effect of releasing ever greater waves of nostalgia. The simple pleasures of the sixties and seventies became the raw materials for a minor industry engaged in mining the past for the pleasures of the eighties and nineties. What had been the background noise of the earlier decades became the forefront of a new branch of entertainment: the packaging of the past. With the aid of long-playing discs and tapes, record stores sold whole days of radio and TV broadcasting from the "Sunshine Decades," as the fifties through the seventies came to be called. People bought week-long blocks of network broadcasting with all the news and the ads, together with the shows. While hanging around home, they bathed themselves in the mediated sunlight of America's high classical era of innocence.

The practice began in old folks' homes. Some unsung genius suggested that the aged residents might enjoy it if the Musak were replaced by programming that would stimulate fond memories. The radio archives of the late forties and early fifties were raided for tapes of Stella Dallas, Arthur Godfrey, and Don MacNeil's Breakfast Club. Soon the search spread to newscasts and the Hit Parade. Eventually they realized that what was wanted was not simply a few "blasts from the past" — the phrase used when replaying the "golden oldies" during the earlier nostalgia wave. Instead, the elderly wished total immersion in the reality of yesteryear. While it was understandable enough that the old might want to return to the atmosphere of their youth, more remarkable were the reactions of the young who visited the old folks' homes. As those environments more successfully simulated the realities of earlier decades, they began to attract people supposedly in the prime of life. Visitors did not want to leave when visiting hours were over. Preretirees competed to take up residence in these refuges from the present.

Just as the cult of youth had characterized the sixties, so the nineties witnessed a cult of age. The senior citizens became the trendsetters for the return to the past that they knew best. Where the bulk of the population had been weighted toward the low end of the age spectrum in earlier decades, now the demographic bulge had slipped toward senescence.

Meanwhile, the young, who could not hope to compete with their more knowledgeable elders at recreating the relatively recent past, reached back even further for their escapes from the dreadful present. Fashions in dress reflected a new fascination with history. Edwardian collars, powdered wigs, waist-pinching corsets, even bustles, made a comeback.

The ultimate combination of nostalgia and decadence came with the retrieval, during the nineties, of those *fin de siecle* fashions from precisely one and two centuries earlier. From the years of Thermidor, beginning in 1795, the last years of the twentieth century borrowed the Parisian habit of wetting down tight-fitting muslin garments to make them even more revealing. From the 1890s, wealthy women of the 1990s borrowed the affectation of piercing their nipples for the insertion of gold rings or jeweled pins. The pierced cheeks and nostrils of the Punks two decades earlier were tame harbingers of barbarities to come.

In 1995, President Milbergs was accused of receiving advance information of large oil reserves on Native American lands in the Southwest, information which he capitalized on by buying leases in the area through his family-owned West States Development Corporation. The charges never reached formal levels and later the press tired of reprinting them over and over. Milbergs responded personally by accusing his accusers of fomenting additional national strife by questioning the credulity and integrity of the highest office in the land. As violence erupted again in 1996, Milbergs invoked emergency powers and threatened to cancel the November elections until national order could be restored. Milbergs was re-elected because his opponent was killed in a campaign plane crash at O'Hare Airport due to a computer error. In order to pay for additional security forces, the budget for the Department of Health and Human Services was cut by 30 percent, a cut which included most Medicaid payments and most federal support of schools past the ninth grade. Funding was shifted to vocational schools; and government research grants, except in the area of defense, were severely curtailed.

In 1998, for the first time in thirteen years, there was real economic growth according to government indices. Although small, a mere 2/10ths of 1 percent, it was greeted as the long lost corner which the country was now turning, the first sign of hope. Last year, growth declined by 3 percent.

If we continue down the road toward the Official Future but encounter severe dislocations on the way, one set of responses would lead to increased social conflict and chronic breakdown, because competitive and selfish values would prevent equitable sharing of an obviously diminishing pie. Under those circumstances, the highly technical and interdependent networks of modern civilization would break down faster than our ability or will to maintain them. A cumbersome and centrist government would create a highly virulent form of the "English disease" with all parties claiming primacy. Fierce protection of turf would lead to conflict, loss, and dehumanization. Although individual decisions can be rationalized within the bounds and needs of "survival," the collective result is less than the sum of its parts. We become as small as we think, individuals with no sense of transcendence or effacement. Chronic Breakdown is not the seedy decadence of Rome, it is the decay of the imagination.

From time to time in a people's history there arise moments of dramatic change. Such moments of revolution are usually produced within the fertile ground of crisis. Perhaps the downward trajectory of economic decay and social disorder may bring us to that kind of crisis. The return to spiritual life that marked the end of the seventies may be a sign that in the face of crisis people may turn toward less secular directions for answers.

Table 9
Statistics: Chronic Breakdown

	1980	2000
World Population (in millions)	4,500	5,921
U.S. Population (in millions)	226	253
World GNP (in billions)	7,000	10,000
U.S. GNP (in billions)	2,600	2,926
U.S. Per Capita Disposable Income	8,100	7,600
U.S. Per Capita Consumption Expenditures	7,400	7,100
Average World Energy Prices ($/bbl crude)	35	40
Energy Consumption (quads)	78	78
Energy Supply by Source (quads)		
Domestic Oil	20	15
Imported Oil	15	7
Shale Oil	0	1
Natural Gas	20	14
Coal	17	32
Conventional Nuclear	3	4
Nuclear Breeder	0	0
Solar, Hydropower, and Other	3	5
Percentage of Income Spent On		
Housing	21	24
Food	21	25
Clothing	8	5
Medical Care	10	5
Transportation	15	10

Note: 1 quad = 10^{15} Btu/yr; all dollar figures are in 1980 dollars.

Table 10
Trends: Chronic Breakdown

No one grows much; the countries surviving best are:

Norway	U.S.S.R.
Brazil	Canada
South Africa	France
United States	

The countries faring poorest are:

Indonesia	Jamaica
Mexico	Nigeria
United Kingdom	Uganda
Netherlands	Ethiopia
Italy	

Occupations which are rapidly growing in demand:

Repairmen of all sorts	Paraprofessionals
Skilled craftsmen (machinists)	(legal and medical)
Farmers	Disc jockeys
Security guards and police	Coal miners
Soldiers	

Occupations which are shrinking in demand:

Airline pilots	Librarians
Aerospace engineers	Lawyers
Secretaries	Managers
Technicians	Bank tellers

Businesses which are growing:

Coal companies	
Repair shops	Radio and TV
Handtools	Hardware stores
Bicycles	Farming

Businesses which are contracting:

Aerospace	
Airlines	Specialty chemicals
Automobiles	Big construction
High technology	Steel
	Forest products

Chapter VII

Apocalyptic Transformation

Human transformation is possible. We see it, albeit rarely, among individuals. But what about the transformation of a whole society? Can a people change direction like a flight of birds, all at once? Would there have to be a leader? Or might some series of events unite all humanity against some common enemy or for some common goal? We like to think that social transformation is an easy thing, an unavoidable elevation just in the offing. But we think it more likely that only a severe shock to the entire system will initiate anything worthy of the word, transformation. *So this scenario illustrates a monumental wave of drastic change, from breakdown through trough toward a crest of transformation. Human transformation* is *possible, even in its social form. But the easy routes toward it are even less likely than the hard ones, which, by their own accounts, are sometimes called miracles.*

O N OCTOBER 9, 1987, the main computer at the NASDAC headquarters in Colorado Springs reported that three Voshkod 10 capsules had broken free from the Soviet Salyut VII space station. Computers quickly calculated the new orbit toward which their maneuvers were taking them. The target was clear: in a slightly lower orbit many thousands of miles away drifted the U.S. space shuttle Columbia, launched on an apparently routine mission just the day before. In earlier days such a rendezvous in space heralded international amity. Now this unannounced approach threatened doom. Unknown to most of the world, including most Americans and Russians, the arms race had spread to the freezing night of space. The Columbia was carrying out the first full-scale test of the Super High Energy Laser (SHEL) to be used as a defense against Russian intercontinental missiles. The Voshkods moving toward the Columbia were part of a new Soviet operational anti-satellite system. Each Voshkod was armed with a missile tipped by a 24 megaton warhead. Even a near miss would destroy an enemy satellite. Once again the Russians had compensated for lack of finesse with brute force.

As the Voshkods moved in to fire the first volley in the first battle in space, the President, who was entertaining the Japanese Ambassador and the press corps in the Rose Garden, got the news from his chief aide. Members of the media watched as the President turned ashen. Visibly shaken, he left without a word. Limousines, military vehicles, and helicopters appeared within minutes. Amidst the shouted queries of reporters, the President was whisked away to Andrews Air Force Base. Within minutes all wire services carried the story that military preparations were underway at the highest levels of government. For lack of any concrete details, the first hour's reports repeated over and over the single fragment of news: the President's plane, a special plane to be used only during war, had taxied out on the runway at Andrews. As the rumor of an impending nuclear attack spread, the nation panicked.

The years leading up to the Voshkod Crisis were hard years, bleak for many. Inflation soared into hyperinflation. Despite all efforts at conservation, exploration, and alternative forms of energy, the nation was more reliant on OPEC oil in 1987 than it had been in 1980. Americans regarded the 1984 OPEC meetings as a new Versailles. Just as the inflation-ravaged citizens of the Weimar Republic had been driven into a collective rage by the reparations payments demanded by the Versailles Treaty ending World War I, so the oil consumers of the world came to resent

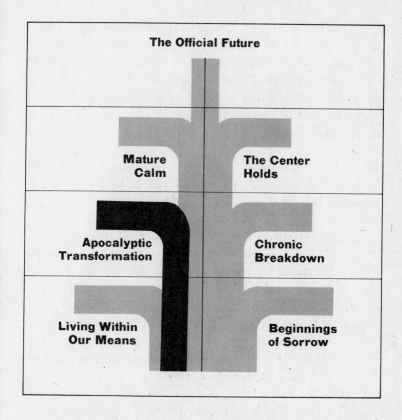

The Official Future

Mature
Calm

The Center
Holds

Apocalyptic
Transformation

Chronic
Breakdown

Living Within
Our Means

Beginnings
of Sorrow

paying reparations for the sins of a dead Shah. The American people suffered a profound resentment at seeing their national net worth drained into the coffers of countries whose mobs shouted anti-American slogans.

Because American industry, particularly agribusiness, had become so energy intensive, rising oil prices had a punitive effect on every man, woman, and child. For every 10 percent increment in the cost of energy there was a 20 percent increase in the cost of food, a 20 percent increase in the cost of machinery, and a 15 percent increase in consumer goods. As incomes dwindled, unemployment increased. Giant corporations that could pass on their inflationary costs to consumers continued to amass capital and pour it back into capital-intensive projects that required

109

fewer workers and more energy. Huge borrowing by both government and business further eroded the dollar and left the lower and middle classes holding the bag for subsidizing limited pockets of capital-intensive economic growth. By the mid-eighties the polarization of wealth and poverty had become clear to all. Most Americans felt impoverished by the combined penalties of inflation, taxation, resource scarcity, and a venal corporate and public policy. Citizens who had long supported law and order and the legislative process now turned bitter. Hard work looked like a dead end. The people who seemed to be getting ahead embodied the worst of human traits: avarice, greed, pride, vanity, and lust. Virtue fell into disfavor.

The hard years drove many to religion, some with a vengeance. Some of the fundamentalist sects bred a passionate opposition to Islam. This reactive fanaticism had the paradoxical effect of importing the culture of the *jihad,* the Holy War, precisely in the attempt to oppose Islam. The call for another crusade to liberate the heathens from the evils of Islam found little favor with the growing Black Muslim movement. Oakland erupted in early 1986. By summertime, religiously motivated guerilla warfare spread to the back streets of Baltimore.

Appalled by the acts of religious fanatics, but needy for spiritual consolation, most people turned to the churches that were closest to them, culturally, socially, and geographically. The horrendous winter of 1986, following years of on-again, off-again drought, accentuated a kind of Biblical ambience. A series of best-selling books turned all the talk about the end of the world into fast profits for large publishing houses.

Into this milieu of apocalyptic doom appeared Malcolm Sean Essend, a rancher and one-time businessman from Bozeman, Montana. It was to Malcolm Essend that the vast majority of people listened during the Voshkod Crisis. It is to Essend that many of today's religions owe their resurgence. Some will argue that we owe the continued existence of our country to him.

Floundering in its sense of failure and doubt, America acted nervously overseas. Saber rattling toward the oily crescent of the

Middle East competed with charges and countercharges hurled back and forth between Russia and the United States. Both Russia and America faced similar socioeconomic problems within their own borders: rising prices, dwindling incomes, soaring food costs, and scarcer resources. Both governments experienced a similar need to posture for the citizenry, if not to take their minds off domestic troubles, then to channel internal frustrations away from real political change. Each year brought the two nations closer to war. The legendary clock on the cover of *The Bulletin of the Atomic Scientists* stood poised for years at one minute to midnight. The final SALT III Treaty failed in the Senate. Domestic attempts to ease the arms race fell into derision. Contacts between Russia and the U.S. became tense and perfunctory. Despite the fact that there were no broken agreements, no disputed territory, and no outright provocations, political exigencies demanded that both countries act out the part of enemies. When actions and perceptions merged into one, as was inevitable, the world fairly crackled with tension.

In addition to the political and economic vicissitudes of the eighties, the specter of pestilence accelerated the movement toward religion. Like the Black Plague in the fourteenth century, experienced by many as a visitation from a punishing God, the pandemic spread of cancer left hardly a family untouched. Whether or not they contracted cancer themselves, people suffered from the sorrow of caring for loved ones. Doctors identified a stress-related syndrome caused by anxiety and apprehension over the possibility of cancer, so ubiquitous had the disease become. Research into the environmental causes of cancer drove millions toward attempting healthier, less polluted lifestyles. Haunted by memories of using products containing asbestos, of working in factories with toxic solvents, of diets rich in chemicals, or of some unknown agent that they never saw, felt, or touched, people came to value nature, wilderness, fauna, the oceans, and all unspoiled environments as sanctuaries from the malignancy of the man-made world. The turn away from synthetic environments and the movement toward religion

111

reinforced one another. Thus the move toward a simpler life drew converts from three distinct but related sources: the failing economy, the rise in disease, and the turn from secular values toward religious values.

Against this turbulent backdrop, Essend appeared quietly on the national scene. Reports of his ministry, if that is a fair description, were primarily restricted to small religious publications with limited circulation. Essend gave talks once a day at a small hall in Bozeman. As the word spread, people would travel from distant states to sit and listen. Ranchers, college students, office workers, housewives, and teenagers came.

As attendance grew, friends hired larger halls. As the crowds grew, Essend seemed to get more serious, quieter, even slightly stern. Eyewitnesses reported that his early talks had been spiced with country folklore and plains humor. But as his reputation grew, Malcolm Essend began every talk with the words "Let us pray." Each prayer was as original and new as that day; the prayers extended for the whole of the talk.

Unlike many of the religious movements that arose during the seventies and eighties, Essend had no church and refused all offers of money. Those who organized the talks, the halls, and the economic tasks necessary to support them, financed the affairs quietly and discreetly. They made it clear to the press that there was no relationship between Essend and their support activities.

Those who returned to other states carried with them stories of their experience, of Essend and a calming Christian movement that seemed to be growing. Former attendees held discussion groups and meetings, always organized by the individuals, with no ongoing contact with Essend. If Essend could be said to be charismatic, it was a uniquely American and even Western form of charisma. Good-looking, over fifty, with a deeply etched, craggy face, he was both soft-spoken and virile, at once the patriarch but devoid of its stereotypes. He spoke with perceptibly deep convictions. Despite the nightly talks, his strong and profound Christian faith never regressed into rhetoric or dogma.

As the media began to investigate Essend, leaders from other religions, churches, and fundamentalist movements visited. There were offers of pulpits, tours, facilities, and willing audiences. But Essend stayed in Bozeman, mostly at his ranch. He was scrutinized constantly by the press, particularly Eastern journalists who remained uneasy and skeptical. The few biographical reports were sketchy. Since Essend never spoke of his background and did not give interviews, his history had to be pieced together.

Essend was born in Idaho in 1930. His parents were farmers, and he attended public schools. When he was a teenager, his family moved to Montana. After attending Montana State University and receiving a degree in agronomy, Essend took a series of odd jobs on ranches and farms near his family in Bozeman. Drafted into the Korean War, he was decorated for bravery on two occasions after he went into enemy fire without regard for his own life to carry wounded companions back to safety. After the war he returned to his father's farm and stayed there following his father's death. His mother died several years later, in 1964, and Essend then lived alone growing wheat and raising cattle. People said that when he wasn't ranching, he was either reading or taking long hiking trips into the mountains. In 1970, Essend sold most of his land and all of his animals. He opened up a small hardware store. Within a year he sold the store. Several weeks after that he rented his small house and left the Bozeman vicinity. That was in 1971. There were reports of his staying in Seattle for several weeks. After that there is no record of his whereabouts for the next nine years. Rent checks were sent to a bank trust he set up, but none of the monies were used during his absence. Friends never received word from him, nor did he tell anyone where he was going. By 1980 it was assumed that he was either dead or in trouble and never coming back. Rumors have it that he spent time in Japan, Thailand, India, Greece, and Israel, although there is no confirmation other than the fact that a passport was issued to him in Seattle in 1971 and renewed in 1976.

In 1981, Essend returned to Bozeman and his house. The talks began at home with a few friends and did not occur in a public hall until almost two years later. Between his talks, Essend read, worked with a few animals he kept, gardened, and grew wheat on land he had once sold but rented back.

By 1985, weekend attendance at the talks had swelled to 20,000. Essend seemed troubled by the crowds, the hoopla, and the organizational tasks involved in what was once a talk with friends. In the middle of that year, just when his popularity and fame had reached a new peak, he stopped speaking for six months. He once again took up his habit of taking long hikes into the mountain wilderness. On Christmas Eve the same year, Essend began his talks again, only now they were on radio, carried by stations across the country, including some of the networks. Deliberately eschewing television, the talks continued on radio for the next year, and then stopped at Christmas, 1986. His only public appearances during this time were unannounced and sporadic, probably in order to avoid the crowds that seemed to trouble him. Nevertheless, people continued to journey to Bozeman. By 1986 these included intellectuals, well-known writers and personalities, movie stars, and avowedly secular persons who felt or sensed in Essend a sincerity of belief and conviction that moved them in unexpected ways. Essend did not create "born-again" Christians with "RAPTURE" bumper stickers, endlessly quoting scriptures. Most people influenced by him seemed deeply touched, as much by his words as by his life and example. People were drawn to Essend's pervading quality of calmness and peace, especially as the world itself seemed drawn into chaos.

During the winter of 1986, Russia began marching toward Baluchistan and the Abadan oil fields, only recently restored to full production since the Iraqi war. This action followed increasing tension between NATO and the Soviets due to Russian insistence that East Germany discontinue unification talks with West Germany. Chinese troops engaged in their most serious conflict to date on their northern border. Soviet troops had invaded at the Dzungarian Gate, using tanks and anti-personnel weapons on the Chinese troops. On the Pacific, the seizure of Japanese fishing trawlers had Japan, Korea, and the U.S. vigorously protesting Soviet extension of its maritime boundaries. Russia seemed to have reached its most irritable and unpredictable state. While Russia saw itself surrounded by an increasingly hostile world, the world saw itself threatened by an increasingly hostile Russia. Stories coming from Russia reported that there were severe shortages of meat, butter, and staples like cooking oil. Embassy officials in Moscow reported long queues at bakeries. There were unconfirmed reports of internal sabotage by Shiite Muslims at the Azerbaidzan oil fields.

At home the fourth credit crunch in eight years coincided with the worst winter in eighty. With low oil stocks and soaring interest rates, financial liquidity reached its lowest point, both for individuals and for corporations. Defaults in small savings and loan institutions were followed by bankruptcies of restaurants, stores, supermarkets, and small manufacturing concerns. The rash of bankruptcies would have become a torrent had the government not extended loans through the newly reconstituted Reconstruction Finance Agency.

Meanwhile the price of gold soared as riots in Soweto threatened to engulf South Africa in a protracted racial war. Mideast tensions, chronic oil shortages, Russian bellowing, and near economic chaos in financial markets drove people into panicky financial decisions. At gold's peak of $2,255 an ounce, people weren't sure whether to sell their fillings and get cash, or sell their possessions to buy gold. They did both in a state of rapid and utter confusion. Thefts increased, silver disappeared from china cabinets, hearing aid batteries were stolen from the ears of the elderly (each contained $50 worth of silver), and jewelry stores bolted their doors and posted signs: By Appointment Only.

Somehow, despite the volatility and madness of the times, the rich bought ever more assiduously on the Fifth Avenues and Rodeo Drives. Opulent stores with astronomically priced goods seemed to goad the world with the message that the wealthy were unaffected by its travails. As 1987 began, the chaos worsened.

Canada nationalized its oil industry, including assets of American companies. The worst earthquake in 140 years struck San Bernardino County, California, killing 14,000 people and causing over $15 billion worth of damage. To compound the misery, summer hurricanes from the Gulf of Mexico lashed furiously and repeatedly at Southern California, causing widespread flooding, crop damage, blackouts, and mudslides. There was civil war in the Philippines when the wife of Ferdinand Marcos took power after his assassination. Financial markets became increasingly skittish, with stocks, bonds, and commodities moving in wide and huge swings that confounded financial planning. The seemingly interminable Midwestern drought created dustbowl-like conditions in Nebraska, Iowa, and Colorado. America threatened military intervention if Russia interfered with the East and West German unification talks. Russian troop movements spread westward to the border of East Germany. NATO forces were put on alert in Germany and the Benelux countries. Because of mismanagement and rumored fraud, the Vatican became partially insolvent and the Pope had to issue an emergency plea to all dioceses for funds. Gene-spliced bacteria formulated for converting algae and seaweed into acetone were found in the Connecticut River. Inflation topped 34 percent. More and more people went to church.

During this time, Essend appeared at impromptu talks given at different churches in the Bozeman area. Pirate tapes and transcripts of his talks were distributed throughout the United States. Visitors pressed him with questions about the world, its future, and their fears. Essend refused to speak directly to issues. His answers were clear but always in parables or allegories. He never mentioned a name, he never mentioned an event. He worked every day. He sold his wheat in town. He kept back 10 percent and gave it to a charity for the hungry.

By the fall a feeling of frenzy filled the air. Foodstuffs disappeared in sporadic waves of panic buying. The army called up its reserves in late September. Troop transports carried battalions to Europe and the Middle East. Banks suffered runs on savings deposits. On September 21, Essend once again allowed his talks to be broadcast nationwide — again for no fee. On the first night about 80 million listened in, the next morning 60 million, and by the following evening fully 100 million were hanging on every word. Essend had become the most powerful person in America. Many smalltown churches broadcast his live talks on Sunday morning in addition to the local sermon. Radios in factories, dormitories, and buses were dialed to his talks.

In the days immediately prior to October 9, the first of the Days of Dread, people were of two moods. One was despair, a seizure of spirit and emotion, a knot-in-the-stomach tension that permeated all of society, all decisions, all activities. The second was paradoxically opposite: a sense of relief, of surrender, of unity with self, family, one's community, and society. People were suddenly sober, thoughtful, and genuinely reflective. As if in a kind of prophetic reckoning of accounts before the final judgment, people exchanged apologies for past wrongs, acknowledged debts left unpaid, and offered assistance to those most in need. Clannishness, individuality, and vanity seemed utterly absurd under the circumstances. With a sense of nostalgic patriotism, people contemplated war and the destruction of their land, history, and culture. While some fled to new locations, migrated, or simply moved to country homes, the vast majority wanted to stay where they were. Although the government did not discuss nuclear war with the American public, it had been manifestly clear in previous policy statements that the United States would use whatever means appropriate to keep Europe and the Middle East free from Soviet aggression, to preserve national sovereignty, and to obtain supplies of oil.

It was 10:02 A.M., EST, when the first report was received at the White House that morning of October 9, 1987. Californians woke to bad news. Within minutes the phone lines of America were tied up. Soon the freeways were as busy as the phone lines as people tried to get back to their families or leave the cities. Even thirteen years later we lack a full account of what happened in the ensuing hours of panic. Much of the information is classified.

But we know that the President left the White House with the knowledge that three armed Soviet spacecraft were maneuvering to attack the Columbia.

The Voshkods were smaller, less sophisticated, and less powerful versions of the space shuttle. Each was armed with a Forager missile. Unless the Columbia was ordered to begin evasive maneuvers, it would be vulnerable to nuclear annihilation within an hour. Or the Columbia could test its new laser on the Voshkods. Either the Columbia's laser cannon destroyed all three Voshkods, or at least one of the missiles would destroy the Columbia. The President knew the stakes were higher than the fate of the space shuttle or its crew of four. The victor could thereafter deny access to outer space to the loser. The denial of critical early warning and intelligence systems would amount to a very real strategic advantage for the winner.

The President ordered the Columbia to counterattack. He reasoned that the Columbia had to defend itself against Russian provocation. Furthermore, the casualties would be few in the sterile void. A nearly bloodless war fought by a few men in space was far preferable to the surface war that might follow if the Russians were to gain a decisive strategic advantage. The President announced from his airborne command post that a secret crisis was underway, but that there was no cause for panic. The U.S. would prevail.

In the complex chess game of orbital maneuvers, the more advanced control systems of the Columbia found a course that could temporarily elude any of the Voshkods and their missiles. The Voshkods, now 500 miles apart after leaving the Salyut, came into daylight one by one hundreds of miles above the Pacific. A few minutes later the slowly rotating Columbia caught the first light of day on its white wings. The great clamshell doors that covered the huge bay slowly opened. The SHEL cannon, a complex collection of gas-tubing and electronic control systems, unfolded like a spiny insect stretching its legs.

The Voshkods detected the change in the attitude of the shuttle. They armed their missiles and began evasive maneuvers.

But a laser beam moves with the speed of light. In less than 2.2 seconds the laser fired three times. The SHEL cannon swung slightly on its mount between each shot as the microcomputer on board retargeted it. In an instant the first burst crossed the thousands of miles that still separated the shuttle from the trio of Voshkods. The instruments on board registered that a laser blast had hit the first Voshkod. Within a millisecond of the laser's impact, the fully armed 24-megaton warhead detonated, blossoming into a ball of plasma that stretched highly energized gas and intense radiation into a distorted lozenge, hundreds of miles in diameter. All radar and visual contact with the other two Voshkods was lost in the dense cloud of blinding radiation. Within minutes, brilliant waves of Aurora Borealis washed through the predawn skies to the west, with a hellish rainbow of radioactive glow.

After ordering the counterstrike, the President, who professed to be deeply influenced by Malcolm Sean Essend, phoned Essend in Montana. Essend's talk that morning was chillingly prophetic, and it was the first talk that ever spoke directly to current events. In the talk, Essend spoke of what it means to be a Christian person, and what it means to be a Christian nation. His prayer was utterly lacking in bellicosity or righteousness. Essend spoke of Russia with empathy and described true Christian virtues as compassion, sacrifice, faith, a generosity of heart, and a welcoming of grace. These virtues were, in Essend's October 9 talk, beyond race, beyond country, culture, or even time. And he added that the world would never perish. Precisely what the President and Essend discussed that day has never been revealed. By noon that day, interrupting the Conelrad broadcasts, Essend was on the radio with his now familiar, "Let us pray. . . ."

His talks continued off and on for the next forty-two hours of mystery amidst utter confusion. The President closed all financial markets and restricted all bank withdrawals to $100 per day per account. Radio stations were no longer on alert, but none knew what to play. Music seemed dissonant under the circumstances. News was almost totally speculative, except news of traffic conditions, gas lines, and an apocalyptic feverishness throughout the populace.

On October 9, the first space war announced itself to the human species with a light show more spectacular and more deadly than any in human history. But the awesome display was only a prelude of what was to come. For the next thirty-six hours the slowly dissipating cloud rotated above the earth as the world waited to learn its source. Hour after hour the planet remained poised in a sense of peril that had no expression, no voice, and no way of understanding. Pandemonium broke out throughout the world. Riots, religious meetings of hundreds of thousands, looting, martial law, vigils, protests, and entreaties constituted a planetary drama that played beneath an eerie light. All the while Essend addressed his listeners in the same stern but compassionate voice. He told Americans to take care of their families, to work, and to pray. Most did.

All wondered what had happened. During this time the whereabouts of the President remained secret. On October 11, in a televised speech from the Oval Office, the President announced that an undeclared and unnecessary war had ended. The United States had won the war in space. Access by free nations to space would be preserved by the supremacy of American technology. He apologized to his people for the secrecy, but he was sure they would understand. He did not tell the people that the first signs of radiation sickness had already begun to show up in the crew of the Columbia who had been bathed in a pulse of intense radiation from the blast. But the astronauts were not the final casualties of the American "victory."

A few hours later the radar screens at Colorado Springs showed that the President had spoken too soon. A faint echo signaled the presence of one of the Voshkod capsules. A few minutes later the second Voshkod's echo came back from the dissipating cloud. Hasty calculations indicated that both Voshkods would fall to earth within thirty-six to forty-eight hours, but the computers were unable to pinpoint the most probable trajectories. The President quickly informed the Soviet Premier. Both agreed that they should inform the world because some other nation would soon detect the surviving Voshkods. They were already too late. "Damocles come true," began the bulletin from a British observatory.

The carriers of death became known as V-1 and V-2. Over each succeeding hour the zone of possible impact for the Voshkods became narrower. One area after another was released from the death sentence until it became clear that V-1 would fall somewhere between thirty and sixty degrees north — that great temperate band within which the majority of the human race lives. As a horrified populace waited, the impact point narrowed. But even minutes before impact no one knew what piece of earth would know Armageddon.

Finally V-1 fell from the sky above the Sea of Marmara, fifteen miles from the Bosporus where Istanbul, earlier Constantinople, and still earlier Byzantium, once stood. Millennia of human history were reduced to rubble in the crucible of the fireball. Many months passed before ships could emerge again from the Black Sea.

Even as the news media told the horror story of Istanbul, the death watch on V-2 continued until early the next morning. In the waning hours it looked as though V-2 would strike in a relatively uninhabited region of Canada. Only a few people saw the mushroom cloud rise far out to sea off Newfoundland. Other nations reacted to the twin calamities with outrage. Within the week the heads of state of over one hundred nations met in Tokyo and demanded the presence of the Soviet Premier and the President of the United States, who were then presented with the Tokyo accords: that each of the superpowers should surrender .5 percent of GNP for the next twenty-five years as reparations, and that they act immediately to initiate nuclear disarmament. As the heads of state met, the final act of the nuclear space war revealed further consequences of America's "bloodless victory."

The huge blast in space had shredded a part of the delicate ozone layer that shields life on earth from the sun's ultraviolet radiation. No one knew how long the damage would last, and as the damage spot drifted over the earth, dancing arrays of iridescent light warned the unwary of the burns and skin cancer they would suffer if they allowed themselves to be exposed to the sun storms. Shortly after the first news of the sun storms reached Tokyo, the Soviet Premier and the President acceded to the accords. The President was deeply troubled by the knowledge that his overestimation of his ability to control the situation had led to such a calamity. The sincerity of his willingness to meet the Tokyo accords was said to be a reflection of the international consensus as well as a sign of how profoundly influenced he had been by Essend.

The sense of relief both at home and abroad was enormous. Grief mixed with joy and gratitude. The emotional outpouring lasted for weeks. In beginning the slow process of reconstructing a new world order, Malcolm Essend was extremely influential, despite the fact that he stopped broadcasting scarcely a month after the Voshkod Crisis. Like the President, he seemed to age greatly the following years. He became reclusive, monkish, and withdrawn. All talks ceased, both in person and by radio. Essendism flourished, of course, but since Essend had never started or favored any one church, Baptists remained Baptists, Catholics continued to be Catholics, and Jews stayed Jews. Yet it was a far less secular country that emerged from the near war.

A new sense of priorities emerged in the early months of 1988. Many heads of corporations announced independently that due to stockholder suggestions and management consensus, future corporate policy would be conducted with community and public advisory boards so that errors of past excesses would not be repeated. Economists spoke out and declared that economic principles had been wrongly divorced from the public good. Politicians talked of reform in their own houses. Several companies suspended manufacture of tactical weaponry. Many smaller subcontractors served notice that they would no longer work on missile or bomber projects.

Prompted by the desire to avoid the continued dependence on OPEC and aided by over a decade of patient research, alternative energy technologies were ready for production on a large scale by the early nineties. A new energy net, decentralized but interconnected, linked solar, geothermal, wind, and hydroelectric generators across the country. Because capital and raw materials were scarce, the effort to rebuild the American economy from the Voshkod Crisis was necessarily labor intensive. The emerging economy drew heavily on local communities and entrepreneurial talent to build new industry. Some of the seeds that had been planted in the counterculture of the sixties finally sprouted in the nineties. The experiments of that earlier decade, sharing and communal living, became in some cases the necessities of the nineties.

Necessity stimulated the recollection of earlier inventions in other realms as well. The nonmaterialistic ethic of Malcolm Essend had opened people's eyes to the development of those resources they could not use up but only increase with use: intellectual disciplines, aesthetic capacities, and, of course, spiritual exercises. The coming to power of a highly religious and Christian society in America did not mean that material gain was altogether eschewed. But it did put into perspective the almost Calvinist association that material welfare had had prior to 1987. By transferring the primary measure of growth and value from the tangible to the intangible, the new ethic relieved the sense of panicked austerity that had inhibited the flow of tangibles and intangibles alike during the eighties. The new ethic offered a hope of solution to the economic depression, not by clever manipulations of the old values, but by a revaluation of value.

During the nineties there arose a new economy of scale, only the scale that turned out to be most appropriate proved to be fairly small rather than very large. For some industries, the most appropriate scale remained very large: industrial redwoods remain redwoods. The very idea of scaling them down to the size of houseplants proved ludicrous. But on the economic forest floor, in the partial shade of the few remaining giant corporations, a secondary growth flourished. Amidst the mottled patches of sunlight that move across the ground as a day passes, a

123

rich ecology of smaller businesses was taking root as the century closed.

All three candidates in the presidential election of 1996 dwelt on the renewal of a sense of hope and promise in America, but not without references to a hard-won sense of prudence and self-reflection. The lasting scars of the protracted recession, the near-war, and the panic that accompanied it were visible everywhere: closed factories, abandoned businesses, overcrowded and decrepit housing. Through the course of two decades the American middle class has slipped from the luxury of choosing lifestyles to the necessity of a more uniform and far more modest standard of living.

The legacy of that week in October and Malcolm Essend is not clear. Essend's frequent emphasis on loyalty seems to have contributed to a level of trust that allows people to govern themselves without high-level machinations among political leaders. Coordination through cooperation replaces coordination by rule. With a formula so simple, and successes so obvious, the people of other nations cannot ignore the lessons, no matter how eager some of their leaders are to maintain the impression of irreconcilable ideologies.

The brush with death and panic has irrevocably humbled and altered the national character. America has taken a more proper role in the world community as a cooperative partner in world development. But most significantly, Malcolm Essend reopened the ground on which individuals practice religion and worship God. Essend's lifelong nonsectarianism proved to many, in this country and around the world, that spiritual value lies not in religious institutions but in personal and faithful practice. America has at least partially restored its own promise to be a land where different people worship differently together.

Of all the scenarios, this is the most speculative and, therefore, least plausible. But the implausibility is the key to its significance, for it revolves chiefly around the notion of transformation, both individual and societal. Our thesis here is that we may move toward rapid social disarray like Chronic Breakdown and find that we require more than gas and hamburgers to satisfy our deeper anxieties. We think it is highly unlikely that we could come even close to such transformation without a correspondingly high level of trauma and crisis. Once transformed, the deeply religious vein of American life could become as dominant as it was at the nation's inception. The degree of prosperity and well-being that exists in our society hides the fact that our very attainment and progress are the firmament upon which rapid social restructuring could occur. With so much to lose and so far to "fall," we are Luciferian in our transitory dimensions. That alone provides a powerful context from which we may know our mortality and, too, our venality. The nature of America's commitment to materiality implies to us that such an awakening would be almost Augustinian in its temporary plunge into darkness. The "dark night of the soul" would be a confrontation with destruction from weapons designed to "save" us. Our enlightenment would be the re-affirmation of life as the final criterion for personal and collective safety.

Mass religious conversions have occurred several times in history. In the sixteenth century, Thomas Münzer led thousands through conversion experiences with profound social implications. The utopian dimensions of Münzer's movement set a theme for philosopher Ernst Bloch's life-long work: a study of the power of hope for the future. In his three volumes on The Principle of Hope, *he shows how an acknowledgment of the openness of the future can liberate the present from the shackles of the past.*

Our next scenario demonstrates the power of hope by showing the disastrous results of thoroughgoing despair. In the face of further deterioration among driving trends, hope turns out to be an important resource, especially when it is scarce. As with the previous two pairs of scenarios, so the final pair demonstrate the importance of individual values in determining different aggregate reactions to similar conditions.

Table 11
Statistics: Apocalyptic Transformation

	1980	2000
World Population (in millions)	4,500	5,900
U.S. Population (in millions)	226	253
World GNP (in billions)	7,000	11,000
U.S. GNP (in billions)	2,600	2,950
U.S. Per Capita Disposable Income	8,100	8,200
U.S. Per Capita Consumption Expenditures	7,400	7,300
Average World Energy Prices ($/bbl crude)	35	100
Energy Consumption (quads)	78	80
Energy Supply by Source (quads)		
Domestic Oil	20	19
Imported Oil	15	6
Shale Oil	0	1
Natural Gas	20	16
Coal	17	20
Conventional Nuclear	3	8
Nuclear Breeder	0	0
Solar, Hydropower, and Other	3	10
Percentage of Income Spent On		
Housing	21	25
Food	21	26
Clothing	8	5
Medical Care	10	7
Transportation	15	15

Note: 1 quad = 10^{15} Btu/yr; all dollar figures are in 1980 dollars.

Table 12
Trends: Apocalyptic Transformation

Countries growing economically: *

Japan	China
Germany	Canada
France	Switzerland
Taiwan	Italy

Countries contracting economically: **

Chad	Zaire
Angola	Indonesia

Occupations which are rapidly growing in demand:

Clergymen	Mediators
Healers	Repairmen
Counselors	Writers
Organic farmers	

Occupations which are shrinking in demand:

Fast-food operators	Bankers
Soldiers	Pornographers
Astronauts	

Businesses which are growing:

The Church	Personal growth centers
Solar energy	Repair
Small-scale production	Crafts

Businesses which are contracting:

Entertainment	Banking
Luxury goods	Machine tools
Weapons sales	Law

*Top 10 percent in growth of GNP 1995-2000
**Bottom 5 percent in growth of GNP 1995-2000

Chapter VIII

Beginnings of Sorrow

Beginnings of Sorrow portrays our worst fears short of nuclear disaster. We confront the Latter Days, the Great Tribulation. That such a future should happen is unthinkable, and yet it is a distinctly possible scenario. We dare not plan for it. Yet we cannot remain oblivious of its threat.

What distinguishes this scenario from Chronic Breakdown is an overwhelming failure of nerve. Though we are hard pressed to see a brighter future in Chronic Breakdown, we do see a future. In Beginnings of Sorrow, national and international events combined with individual and social responses lead a critical mass of people to believe and act as though there would be no future. Such beliefs and subsequent activities profoundly affect the options available to our society. A narrowness of vision restricts our collective potential to mere survival. Where there is a stubborn resistance to events in Chronic Breakdown, the citizenry of Beginnings of Sorrow panic. Lootings, epidemics, banditry, and anarchy are supposedly not the stuff of which Americans are made. But in this scenario America faces its severest test and fails. Suddenly the richest nation the world has ever known goes broke. Virtually everyone feels victimized. Cold weather, crime, hunger, and abandoned institutions leave an angry, weakened, and shocked populace that experiences a psychic death. In this scenario we put all of our eggs in one basket, the basket of a high-growth, energy-dependent industrial society. That basket topples from the perch of our high expectations.

How could this happen? Problems like energy, inflation, crime, and moral decay may yet overwhelm our capacity to solve them. The crises we confront may be out of control. All of our past follies may catch up with us as heedless industrial folly has with the poor citizens who live near Love Canal. We may exhaust hope and replace it with fear. We may learn how thin is the veneer of civilization. The psychology of fear may drive us toward a new Dark Age.

Many people who lived through some of the darker days in Europe following World War II can tell you what it's like to have a nation fall apart. Barbara Tuchman's remarkable study, A Distant Mirror, *shows us what a civilization in chaos can be like. The survivors of Cambodia, E. Timor, or Auschwitz are testaments both to survival and to what humans are capable of inflicting upon each other.*

We Americans assume that somehow we are invulnerable to all that. But we shouldn't forget our own Civil War and its aftermath in the South, or My Lai, or Jonestown. We are a nation that went to the moon, but in that same year we were also killing thousands of Vietnamese with equal technological efficiency.

I T IS STILL TOO DIFFICULT to speak about the past with systematic objectivity. Scenes and impressions tell the story. Four-year-old children cry unattended in vacant suburban shopping centers. Rats skitter among piles of uncollected garbage. People have taken to carrying pistols. Money consists of gold fillings, silverware, and antibiotics.

There is almost no economy. Any corporation that tried to cope was physically trashed by mobs. Most supermarkets and food distribution channels lie in ruins. Farmers have to guard their crops. Adventuresome distributors trade food at urban markets with all the cunning and connivance of pawnshop brokers. Communications have broken down. The nation has broken into ten thousand local feudal economies. Some utilities, unable to collect fees, have shut down. There are rumors of nuclear power plants being abandoned while their cores remain active. We do not really know what is happening in many parts of America. News is by rumor and innuendo. Radio broadcasts are spotty and strangely informed. TV broadcasting is only local. There are no national TV networks because there is no national market. Sometimes the silence is unbearable. Everyone wants to know what is happening.

The suddenness and rapidity with which the social fabric tore caught everyone by surprise. In 1983, an opulent America was borrowing and spending freely. The tumultuous events of the seventies had made us callous and, in the end, myopic. The Carter Doctrine had made it clear to the world that America considered the oil-producing nations of the Middle East "within the sphere of our vital interests." We would go to war for oil as well as for the "protection of democracy." So defense spending soared beyond earlier constraints. The coupling of the threat of communism with the threat of a cutoff in oil supplies rendered the arguments of the military highly persuasive. The Department of Defense went on a buying spree that included tanks, airplanes, killer satellites, neutron bombs, precision-guided munitions, MX missiles, and an expanded corps of personnel. The federal current-accounts budget swelled enormously and the accompanying deficits were brutally inflationary. The false sense of prosperity finally broke the back of the American economy.

The states with large metropolitan areas fared much worse than the Midwestern rural areas. Life has changed relatively little in the Panhandle. Detroit, though, is unrecognizable. The degree to which areas have been able to sustain viable societies is the degree to which they are self-sufficient. Where there are oil refineries, natural gas, and food within close proximity of each other, yet removed from urban areas, strong regional pockets have resisted chaos and mania. For the rest of the country, food requires transportation, and to talk about transportation, one must talk about Black Christmas.

The world had seemed stable in the winter of 1983. But with

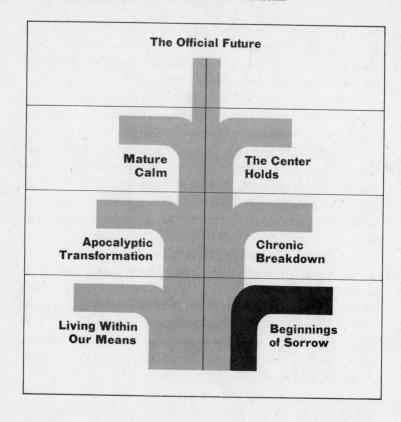

Christmas only two weeks away, terrorists from ten Islamic countries, the League of Popular Forces (LPF), attempted to disrupt the oil life line of the world.

In a series of precisely planned moves they attacked all over the world at once. They crippled oil rigs in the North Sea and Gulf of Mexico; disabled pipelines across Alaska, the U.S., Saudi Arabia, and the Soviet Union; crippled refinery complexes in Philadelphia, Los Angeles and Galveston, all over Europe, Asia and the Persian Gulf; and sunk a mined ship in the Strait of Hormuz. At the end of the day there was still oil in the ground, but the complex, interlocked system that brought oil to its ultimate users was near collapse.

Oil panic erupted. It took over seventy-two hours to assess the damage to the world system, and during those three days every oil company and every oil-producing and oil-consuming nation came to fear that oil would be in desperately short supply in and for the near future. The price of oil skyrocketed in the ensuing rush to buy up remaining stores. Forty-eight hours into the crisis the price of a barrel of crude topped $100. Nearly every gas station in the world had been emptied in the first twenty-four hours. While rich nations bid among themselves for the oil, poor nations threatened further disruptions of the world economy if they were denied the precious stuff.

The first reaction worldwide was to hold back oil supplies. The new relationship between supply and demand caused uncertainty, particularly because the U.S. dollar was inflating at an all time high — 28 percent per year — and oil-exporting nations were not at all certain how to align their governments or their oil with a country that was plunging economically.

At home, most of the oil reserves were seized by the military. Civilian reserves lasted ten weeks. Domestic production was insufficient to maintain any economic growth and, fearing a large scale recession, corporations began massive layoffs and cutbacks. Overnight, spending stopped. There was a run on banks and thrift institutions as individual depositors tried to accumulate cash, food, and supplies. With uncertainty running so high, hoarding began in all commodities. As the tax base shrank, the government began issuing large amounts of currency in order to support its military expansion in the Middle East. This fiat money, immediately viewed with contempt, exacerbated the problem of hoarding as merchants and suppliers increasingly refused to be paid in dollars. The rush to convert cash to survival-type assets accelerated until the government declared a banking holiday on Friday, October 10, 1984, closing all institutions until currency restrictions could be agreed upon.

At this point, the unraveling of U.S. society became so complex and interactive that newspapers could not keep abreast of the news. On Monday, October 13, 1984:

"Utah today closed all its borders to traffic except for incoming and outgoing commercial carriers. The Governor cited security and safety of its citizens as reason. Only those with valid Utah addresses were allowed in. The federal government has brought suit and threatened to use the National Guard to reopen Interstate 80."

"Roving gangs burned and looted several cities during the weekend as the unseasonably hot Indian Summer continued. TVs, stereos, records, jewelry, and liquor were the main targets of the mobs. Detroit, Cleveland, and Buffalo are under martial law, as is the state of Louisiana."

"Runs on gasoline, kerosene, and batteries have occurred in many areas. Stocks are nonexistent in some. Large outflows of urban residents to summer homes are reported in California, Illinois, and New England. Some are moving their families to outlying areas until the cities calm down."

"Hijackings on highways have been reported. Authorities cannot meet all calls. Trucks have been hit hard and the Teamsters are calling for armed guards on all trucks starting Monday."

"The mayors of thirty cities have called upon the President to invoke a national curfew and to speed food to besieged cities."

"Israel has threatened to use nuclear weapons on the capital cities of Iran, Syria, Jordan, and Saudi Arabia in response to the threatened Holy War on Israel. All military and IAF installations are on full alert."

"Canada has cut off all natural gas shipments to the U.S. until further review of domestic energy policies has been completed."

"Indonesia revoked the licenses of all American companies to its oil and mineral reserves. The President has ordered the carrier Constellation and the Seventh Fleet south from Guam. White House sources made no further comment."

"The government announced today a freeze on all food prices retroactive to October 1. Major food retailers have agreed, but privately, industry sources confide that it will make food even scarcer in time, as producers withhold supplies. The new ceiling prices on some staples are: 24-ounce loaf of bread — $1.75; ½ gallon milk — $2.39; and 1 pound of ground meat — $4.63."

On Tuesday, October 14, 1984, the New York Stock Exchange withheld trading for three hours. The entire market was gap-opened at a discount of 30 percent. Within an hour, the market plunged another 50 percent to 500 on the Dow Jones. Meanwhile, the President announced that the U.S. would purchase all gold held by citizens. After thirty days, all privately held gold could be redeemed at fifty new dollars per ounce. The announcement of a new currency coupled with the seizure of gold collapsed the commodities market except for foodstuffs. Other financial markets closed until agreement could be reached on how to revalue in light of the new dollar.

As layoffs increased, fuel and gasoline problems caused shortages in many consumer goods, particularly foodstuffs. Produce growers in California were unable to ship their winter crops to the East. As prices soared with the shortages, the weather turned bizarre. Frosts killed the citrus crops in the South.

During the winter almost no snow fell in the Midwest. The cold and lack of snow cover killed over 60 percent of the winter wheat crop. By spring it was obvious that food had become a major problem with three distinct causes. Farmers could not obtain fuel or spare parts to plant crops that spring. The food that was available was increasingly difficult to get to market. And shortages were driving up prices at a time when incomes were dropping. Although many people shifted to the most simple and basic of diets and ate white rice, beans, and canned meats when available, even those provisions required good connections or a big wallet. Supermarkets had as many bare shelves as full. Produce sections carried potatoes and local storage crops, but no fruits. The dairy cases were often empty. Herds were slaughtered and sold for hard assets because dairymen could not count on markets, transportation, or even electricity to cool the milk. Glass bottles were available only in some locales. Whiskey sold for as much as $50 a litre.

By the late spring of 1985, the second wave of riots started. Gary, Indiana, was first; and within days, they had spread across the country. Fires, looting, robbery, and armed violence gave the government additional cause to seize resources, particularly fuel, food, and transportation. The confiscations further dried up supplies and forced the citizenry further into scarcity. Producers of oil were under edict to produce to capacity. But the uncertainty in the financial markets caused most to hold back under elaborate ruses and deceptions. The long-term value of oil was now assured, and few were willing to let it go for fiat dollars — new or old. A beefed-up Department of Energy bureaucracy enforced the production rules and became as hated to the oil producers as OSHA was to manufacturers. But the worst feature of the governmental policy was its effect on further development and exploration for energy. Because the government forced production and set prices at the artificially low value of $90 per barrel, investments came to a halt. The steady decline in domestic production accelerated. With the decline in petroleum consumption came the surge in coal. Where it was close enough to be obtainable, everyone burned coal in stoves, fireplaces, factories, even in open pits keeping warehouses above freezing. Some old steam engines returned to the Erie and Lackawanna.

The effects of increased air pollution and short food supplies, coupled with poor nutrition and increased psychological stress from economic duress, caused a rapid decay in the national health. With medicines in short supply it soon became necessary to ration drugs to those who were in greatest need. In most cases those with the money had the "greatest need." The poor and newly indigent were often faced with little or no medical care for their illnesses. The shortages were painful for cancer patients.

Whether it was the coal, the stress, or just a result of timing, the late eighties saw the fuse on cancer burn to its short end. Within ten years, cancer had doubled and then tripled the mortality rate. Particularly appalling was the increase among children. By the tens of thousands, young adults, teenagers, and youngsters fell victim. That cancer was a disease of civilization was known, but that it should flare so violently as civilization buckled was a torment few could understand. It was a common story to hear of whole families falling ill and dying, one by one, first by cancer, then by stroke, then by heart attack, and finally by grief. Curiously, often the grandparents survived.

Running sores and infections were seen on the streets. Antibiotics were available but not well distributed. Strange flus and viruses swept the country. Racking coughs pierced the public silence of buses and open-air markets. Cysts grew on faces and hands. Most pregnancies were terminated. The legacy of toxic wastes forced towns into misery as the wastes continued to be ingested in drinking water or breathed in the air.

By early 1990, the disruption in national markets was so severe that television advertising had dropped to a trickle. With goods in chronic short supply, there was no need to advertise. Two of the networks merged. The third, NBC, sold most of its assets and deeded the system to a government channel. By then there was only the ABC evening news program, and it was watched intently by everyone. The news took on an eerie quality. Its hour-long message was a toll of the casualties, a list of the damage. Most people watched because most were better off than the victims on the news. It was a way of reminding oneself that as bad as things were, at least you were better off than someone else. When the ABC newscasters were attacked by a revolutionary group of Trotskyites and mowed down by heavy gunfire during taping, the American Broadcasting System ceased its nightly news permanently. From that point on, the government became the sole source of news, but these broadcasts were essentially propaganda. In many areas, power outages and transmitter problems eliminated even this source of communication.

The attack on ABC was a signal to thousands of frustrated youth to join the "patriots," better known as "Whiteshirts." Dressed in pseudo-revolutionary garb and educated on slogans, they formed a terrorist paramilitary group that bullied towns and villages across America, all in the name of the Constitution, freedom, and a reunited America. Everywhere they engendered hatred of minority groups and scapegoats with inflammatory slogans. Where food was short, they staged kangaroo trials of supermarket executives. Always found guilty and humiliated, the defendants were beaten, jailed, their families torn apart, their wives raped, their homes ransacked. Jews were favorite targets. In the Southwest, Chicanos suffered most; in California, the Chinese and Japanese. In college towns, professors feared for their lives. In blue collar towns, executives locked themselves and their families behind the closed gates of their factories.

The Whiteshirts grew rapidly. The government made a calculated decision not to suppress them, perhaps because it feared an all-out guerilla war, perhaps because they played into its hands as an effective control of the populace. Perhaps it knew it could not suppress them. In any case the unholy alliance turned the average citizen into both victim and conspirator. It paid to lie and inform. It did not pay to resist or speak out. In some areas the Whiteshirts collected taxes. They also collected an organization levy. In lieu of levies, the Whiteshirts sometimes accepted women as "trainees." Force, humiliation, and pain were their common tools of domination. A ludicrous rhetoric of freedom accompanied the coercion.

Nevertheless some areas resisted both the Whiteshirts and the pervasive nihilism. These pockets of resistance were particularly galling to the Whiteshirts. Certain areas that were geographically unique and relatively sufficient in resources formed their own paramilitary guard through the county sheriff's department. Marin County, Evanston outside of Chicago, the Main Line near Philadelphia, and Shaker Heights near Cleveland, to name a few, stubbornly resisted both the Whiteshirts and the national malaise. Food was rationed and available. Strong interneighborhood groups watched streets at night. The citizenry pooled their assets to form tight pockets of camaraderie and organizational know-how through which all essential services were available and disbursed. That these areas not only survived but thrived without the "help" of the Whiteshirts was a thorn in the group's side. They viewed the idea that citizens and communities could better control their destiny without the Whiteshirts as a heresy and attacked with subversion and infiltration. Communities responded with identification cards, checkpoints, and violence in kind. Businessmen became drill sergeants and commandos. Some confessed that they found the excitement exhilarating. But the thrill was short-lived.

In 1991, the Whiteshirts launched an all out attack on Marin. Escalating far beyond the pretense of orderly trials and random bullying, they came across the Golden Gate Bridge with heavy arms and chemical agents. Despite valiant efforts at hand-to-hand combat, the citizens of Marin were forced to retreat in the face of overpowering arms. Some fled to the north. Those who tried to hide in crude camps on the slopes of Mount Tamalpais were finally swept in toward the Bay by clouds of choking, killing gas released near the ocean to ride inland on the onshore breezes. Marin fell during the Christmas holidays. A shudder of hopelessness spread through the last vestiges of middle-class America.

Since the early nineties, news has become scarce from most areas. Unconfirmed reports claimed that Oregon, Washington, and Idaho were trying to unite with British Columbia to form a stronghold against the Whiteshirts. But there is no way to confirm those reports. In any case, it hardly matters to the rest of the country.

What matters now is today. Very few people enjoy the luxury of planning for tomorrow. The necessities of life demand eighteen hours a day of hard work, vigilance, and a certain cunning. Occasionally, the army will come through and recruit for the wars. According to veterans, there are wars in Mexico, North Africa, Indonesia, China, and, of course, the perennial war in the Middle East. Military service has been a consistent way for the young to be clothed and fed. Some send back money and some are simply sent back with a small check. One of the mothers opened her son's coffin against government orders and reportedly saw a body that looked like an ashen replica. Her fingers went through his chest like a burnt sponge cake. But since we have not heard of any nuclear engagements, we can't be sure what this means.

Many wondered how it was that in light of the near collapse of American society potential predators like the U.S.S.R. had not leapt to deliver a death blow. An aging U.S. nuclear arsenal still posed a real threat to the Soviet Union. The balance shifted against the U.S., but there was still capacity to inflict awesome devastation upon an attacker. Furthermore the Soviets had other problems with which to contend.

In the East, the Chinese-Soviet border was a perpetual stalemated front. Who began the fighting remained unclear, as did its aims. Each victory was temporary. The fighting faded only to flare anew a short time later. Rumors carried tales of biological and chemical warfare and even the use of tactical nuclear weapons.

On the western borders of the Iron Curtain, the situation was more bizarre. Europe had hardly fared better than the U.S. In West Germany, a right-wing regime held together an aging industrial machine in preparation for war. A well-armed Germany stood as barrier to Soviet expansion toward the West. But that did not prevent the Soviets from trying.

By 1986 France had gone fully socialist in its attempt to cope with a collapsing world economy. It exerted strong leadership among the left-wing regimes of southern Europe. That spring the Soviets along with the Warsaw Pact nations engaged in maneuvers that fooled no one. An invasion of West Germany seemed imminent. The U.S.S.R. issued a call to its European socialist brothers to join with them in preventing the rise again of German fascism. But French President Jean Roche flew to East Berlin for a meeting with the heads of state of Eastern Europe. The Russians expected an announcement that France had joined the fold. Instead he called upon the remaining socialist nations to resist Russian imperialism. German nationalism asserted itself as East Germany remained neutral. Anti-Soviet riots in Poland and Czechoslovakia gave their leaders clear signals. Socialism was one thing; Russian imperialism and the risk of WW III another. Bulgaria and Romania remained in the Russian camp, but the Warsaw Pact was as fragmented as NATO.

By the end of the month, Europe was in a new tripartite balance. The better off right-wing nations of northern Europe were well armed but less numerous. They were balanced against the more numerous socialist nations of eastern and southern Europe, led by a nuclear-armed France and a powerful East German war machine. They both stood against the U.S.S.R. and its remaining allies. No war broke out, but an uneasy peace persisted into the next decade. For the U.S., the burden of defending Europe was at an end. It could concentrate on its own borders and problems.

From what news the government issues, and from stories of pilots and nomads, a sketchy picture of America at the millennium emerges. It has managed to retain both its borders and outlying territories, although Hawaii is completely under control of the military and looks more like Guam than a tourist resort. The government is strongest militarily, but it is stretched thin overseas and uses the National Guard only to protect those domestic areas where critical machines and resources are manufactured or stored. Parts of Wichita, Seattle, Orange County, and Houston are heavily guarded and protected since they supply critical war machinery. Jeep production in Toledo is intact, but the River Rouge automobile factories are permanently closed. There is still a GM plant operating in Fremont, California, and one in Alabama, but otherwise, no new cars roll off assembly lines.

Most medium-sized cities have large populations of indigent children running in gangs. During the late eighties, many women gave up their children to agencies. When the agencies reached their capacity and some collapsed under the strain of worsening circumstances, their wards were abandoned to the streets. Some found homes with strangers, many of whom had questionable motives. Now there is no one who will house the orphans. That they survive at all is a miracle. Some polish the black shoes of the Whiteshirts for food rations. Others beg and steal. Some die.

The larger cities function subnormally. Chicago is abandoned downtown. The exodus to the smaller country towns continues in

141

the face of fierce resistance from locals. Small towns boil with new occupants, many housed on the outskirts in shacks made of plastic and scrap lumber. In the country there is food, at least, and sometimes work.

Acid rains in the Northeast stretching to the Great Lakes have left the entire region devoid of most fish life. Forest areas are giving way to brush and thistle. Vegetable crops in summer gardens suffer from the rain. The change in botanical life has reduced insect and bird populations. The blue jay and the robin are no longer seen in New England. The inability of government to enforce EPA restrictions on emissions and effluents has turned our rivers into raw sewers. Municipalities cannot afford the energy expense of treating wastes. The Hudson and Connecticut rivers are smelly, brown, and completely toxic.

Technology and innovation have come to a complete halt. Although the government still produces and orders high-tech military equipment, there are few research facilities operating save for some military-industrial companies. The harsh economic realities have closed many educational institutions as well. Those that have managed to remain open carry on the least expensive of activities: the humanities, the social sciences — and guarding the buildings and museums. Many universities were destroyed in the student riots of 1988. When all federal monies were withdrawn from both institutions and students, violent anti-government and anti-education riots ravaged many campuses. Some were "re-occupied" by dissidents as "free cities" where courses were taught in Marxist and radical thought. The overwhelming problems of everyday necessities brought most educational activities to a halt. The students soon became squatters arguing with each other over petty territorial issues and rights. Within a year Madison, Yale, and Columbia were completely destroyed as educational centers. Books were burned for fuel, furniture broken up for the same reason, and the grounds dug up into crude gardens and plots, some with pigs and chickens. Berkeley looked like any other slum. The students' inability to deal with their eroding social and economic environment was a source of frustration and bitterness.

The fact that their education had been wasted both in terms of gaining professional job status on the one hand and in ill-preparing them for survival skills on the other caused much anguish. Many campuses saw pitched battles between opposing radical movements. Whiteshirts fought Maoists, who in turn opposed Separatists.

In areas as far as fifty miles from major cities, there are no trees. They have been cut down for fuel. Animals are very scarce. Cats and dogs have disappeared. Grazing animals remain only in distant rural areas, usually under twenty-four-hour guard. Rustling is common and once again punishable by death.

As national systems of production and distribution have failed, the government has gained more and more control over our lives and over resources. All petroleum and mining companies have been nationalized. Government workers receive low wages but receive in addition the all-important ration coupons for food, kerosene, diesel fuel, and medicines. These coupons, given in slight excess of normal needs, can be sold or bartered for goods. Most government workers are therefore relatively well off.

As the government controls increase, so does real anarchy. The fact is that the government cannot deal with the job before it. Many of the supervisory personnel are corrupt. Graft is widespread. Bribery is necessary for travel permits. A citizen dependent solely on government rations for food would die within a year. Government controls are ineffective, but just enough to provide an arrogant bureaucracy with both the illusion of control and a means to salt its own larder. Government workers disappear at night into government-owned housing compounds, rightfully afraid to come out at night. There is an unspoken agreement: the government rules by day while the Whiteshirts rule the night.

Now that travel permits are required, though rarely issued, there is no chance of going to the country. Each travel sector is the size of a county and check points are scattered inside. The main reason for the permits is to keep minorities and "undesirables" out of the country. The relative riches of the farmers are creating a new class in many rural areas, and political power has

143

reverted to the farming belts. Since both oil and food are concentrated in these food-producing states, the industrial cities of the Northeast have become anemic in their ability to exercise any control over the army, budgeting, or resources. While many former executives struggle to keep their families alive, dirt farms are becoming quite wealthy. Such stories drive urbanites wild with anger and frustration. Roving gangs of rural farmboys travel the backroads at night and pick up runaways from the cities. Urban refugees are searched, looted, and then handed back to transfer agents. Many a family has tried to flee with what little wealth it could amass, only to be caught, impoverished, and shipped back to the city to find its old house occupied by squatters.

There is much talk prefaced by "If only I had. . . ." Without work and without purpose, people talk idly, speculating on what happened to their lives. It has all happened so fast. No one could imagine how quickly a city as beautiful as San Francisco or Savannah could decay, or how fragile was the American Dream, or more frightening, how superficial the American character. Now that people know, there is nothing they can do about it except dream: "If I had only sold the business and bought the farm when Helen said we ought to, I could have. . . ."

"If only. . . ." That is the refrain of the sorrowful. Even after the shattering of the social compact, people would wonder that such decay was ever possible. If only they had kept it together just a little bit better early on, "Then the dreadful slide into violence and terror never would have happened. If only. . . ."

But what can one do prior to disaster? Before the break one cannot tell how thin is the surface of civilization. The Watts riots started with an attack on a Coca-Cola delivery truck. One by one a lot of people may decide to survive rather than surrender to the increasing numbers of outlaws.

Yet survival values become more useless as driving trends become more adverse. The more rigidly we adopt the lifeboat ethic, the less ably we can cope with radical discontinuity.

144

This scenario presents one way of imagining what happens to a society that is wholly dependent on materialism as its criterion for success. If prosperity should suddenly cease, people may do things that seem unthinkable under other circumstances. They might cease to choose. They might succumb to blind barbarism.

One can observe the seeds of another response to adverse circumstances. The recent movements toward renewable energy sources, organic agriculture, and less technological, bureaucratic, and expensive means of health care may be the laboratories of tomorrow's society. Perhaps The Whole Earth Catalog *is the Sears, Roebuck catalog of the eighties and nineties. Our final scenario shows people coping with driving trends every bit as bad as those in Beginnings of Sorrow. But different values make the difference between the sorrows of, "If only. . . ." and the measured hope of, "Just maybe. . . ."*

Table 13
Statistics: Beginnings of Sorrow

	1980	2000
World Population (in millions)	4,500	5,000
U.S. Population (in millions)	226	226
World GNP (in billions)	7,000	6,500
U.S. GNP (in billions)	2,600	1,180
U.S. Per Capita Disposable Income	8,100	4,000
U.S. Per Capita Consumption Expenditures	7,400	3,900
Average World Energy Prices ($/bbl crude)	35	100
Energy Consumption (quads)	78	40
Energy Supply by Source (quads)		
Domestic Oil	20	15
Imported Oil	15	1
Shale Oil	0	0
Natural Gas	20	10
Coal	17	11
Conventional Nuclear	3	0
Nuclear Breeder	0	0
Solar, Hydropower, and Other	3	3
Percentage of Income Spent On		
Housing	21	35
Food	21	40
Clothing	8	5
Medical Care	10	10
Transportation	15	5

Note: 1 quad = 10^{15} Btu/yr; all dollar figures are in 1980 dollars.

Table 14
Trends: Beginnings of Sorrow

Countries that are, at least, survivors:

Japan	Germany
China	Brazil
United States	Saudi Arabia
Canada	South Africa
Norway	France

Countries that are nearly collapsed:

U.S.S.R.	Angola
United Kingdom	Zimbabwe
Iran	Argentina
Egypt	Ecuador
Turkey	Mexico

Occupations which are growing in demand:

Private police	Craftspersons
Thieves	Handweapons manufacturers
Repairpersons	Blacksmiths
Farmers	

Occupations which are contracting in demand:

Executives	Advertising
Bankers	Teachers
Bureaucrats	Lawyers
Programmers	Scientists

Businesses which are growing:

The Mafia	Farming
Guns	

Almost all businesses are contracting, especially:

High technology	Fast food
Financial services	Leisure

Chapter IX

Living Within Our Means

A radical transformation of society follows from diverse adaptations to a declining economy plagued by shortages of resources. Following the energy crisis of the seventies, the eighties hit with an equally surprising food crisis causing massive dislocation of both individual and world economies. Unlike the survival-oriented ethic of Beginnings of Sorrow, American ingenuity, pluck, and gumption forestall social collapse by a rapid restructuring. Americans do not change because they think change would be better; they change because the old ways no longer work. Middle-class Americans adopt much of the lifestyle pioneered by the counterculture of the seventies, without surrendering more than a few inches to its underlying ideology. The masses of the eighties and nineties meet the privileged drop-outs of the sixties and seventies in a social milieu of a deteriorating climate, severe resource shortages, and a faltering economy. Far from the fruited plain on which their former rivalries were fought, diverse groups establish a common ground of belief that the world has changed irrevocably and in a way that renders frugality, conviviality, cooperation, spirited attention to community, and finally hard work as the last best hope for mere survival.

I N 1982, THERE WERE SIGNS that the economic policies of the new Republican administration were beginning to work. Certainly the psychology had changed. The flow of capital into industry had a salubrious effect on the populace. Stocks

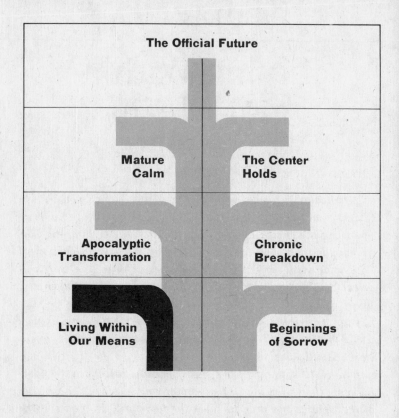

The Official Future

Mature
Calm

The Center
Holds

Apocalyptic
Transformation

Chronic
Breakdown

Living Within
Our Means

Beginnings
of Sorrow

returned to favor, savings increased, and the reduction in interest rates stimulated the housing industry, making more homes affordable. The first tax reduction had not increased inflation, and most people felt they were getting ahead. Unfortunately, few were attending to the worrisome news about food.

Grain stockpiles that had been reduced during the summer of 1980 were not replenished. Although 1981 provided a moderate crop, by the spring of 1983 it was obvious that world stocks of grain had plummeted. China was buying large quantities of rice, the Japanese were accumulating everything, and the Russians were heavy buyers of wheat. With the drought of 1983 cutting United States production by one third, the stockpiling by nations became aggressive. Prices rose continuously for four months but had no effect on demand. Wheat tripled to $12 a bushel. Soybeans hit $18, while corn topped $9 for the first time in history.

In 1984, prices kept climbing. The $1 billion sell-off of gold by the Russians confirmed rumors of a third disastrous harvest in as many years. Before the Russians could buy though, commodities markets began to soar again. A late winter had wiped out most of the Canadian wheat crop, as well as 30 percent of the American crop. Corn and soybeans had shriveled up during the previous summer, bringing feedstocks to their lowest level in thirty years. Before the government could act, the prices of commodities soared into unbelievable ranges. A bushel of wheat was $22. The standard loaf of bread topped $3 in the supermarkets. A bottle of Mazola was $7. Ground round was on special at $5.99 a pound.

The impact of high prices and short supply traveled back and forth through society like shock waves. More than the cost and inconvenience, the half-empty shelves of the supermarket struck at the very quick of America's sense of security. People hoarded, overbought, and stored despite pleas to the contrary. The panic buying made high prices absurd prices, and shortages turned into routs. There was talk of the apocalypse, the four horsemen, of doomsday, and Biblical plagues. Respected agronomists asserted that the world might never recover from the shortages, and the specter of a domestic famine surfaced.

Starvation spread across fifteen countries including India, Bangladesh, Trinidad, Costa Rica, Nicaragua, Chile, and north-east Africa — even America. Instances of deaths caused by mal-nutrition created a sensation in the world press. The news of Americans starving to death was unbelievable. The crisis demon-strated that America, like the rest of the world, had less of a supply problem than a distribution problem. Even in this severest of shortages, there were enough calories to go around. Neverthe-less, dozens of elderly Americans starved to death. America's sympathy for the world's hungry reached an almost pathologi-cally low point; it was too wrapped up in its own problems. Just as fistfights had broken out in gas lines in 1973, Americans did not demonstrate their finest behavior at the onset of the crisis. Crime related to food shortages soared. Pilferage and rustling increased. Guards were posted on fields near harvesttime, and corruption was widespread in the meat business. Rationing did nothing but confuse the matter. Food doubled and tripled in price. But, except for meat and other grain-dependent products, shortages were mainly caused by panic buying. The new price levels were real, and Americans had to adjust to spending more money for foodstuffs. When the dust settled Americans were poorer, but in some ways better fed. The rich fatty foods were cut back in consumption, and like the Danes during World War II, Americans found that high prices and shortages could force them to have better personal health. Farmland tripled in price and made instant millionaires of many. For other farmers, the high price levels provided their first opportunity to get out from a mountain of debt that had been accumulated over two decades of boom and bust farming.

For the President, the run-up in food costs posed sticky political problems. To do nothing would have meant certain defeat in the next elections. To place price controls on food would have alienated party regulars and farmers, who were becoming counterparts to Saudi princes. Stories of irregularities in the commodities market implied that traders' profits were in the multibillions. Ted Kennedy was barnstorming the country and attracting huge crowds. The President seemed confused and frustrated by the situation. The food crises and the administration's inertia convinced the people and the popular press that there was a cabal of food corporations, landowners, grain companies, and financiers who were reaping bountiful profits at the public's enormous expense. The profits of some of the grain companies were as stunning to the American public as the earlier reports of oil companies. Although the President narrowly won re-election, his problems and the problems of America had only just begun. Inflation climbed to the 20 percent level. Within four years, the percentage of disposable income spent on food went from 16 percent to 30 percent. School-lunch programs went broke. Some kids didn't eat all day. Homemakers demonstrated at supermarkets and food processing plants. All food prices rose as demand shifted from one product to the next. The average family of four required $800 per month for food. Many restaurants had to close for lack of ingredients. Menus in others were half crossed out. Consumer spending dropped as families cut back in order to meet their food budgets. Spending for shoes, clothing, records, furniture, and vacations was postponed in favor of food. Tourism plummeted in Hawaii and sent the state into an economic tailspin. The auto industry, which had barely recovered from 1980, collapsed. Ford filed for reorganization under Chapter 11 in 1985. Sears, K-Mart, and other department stores posted record losses while Safeway, Kroger's, and Winn-Dixie saw record profits. Layoffs were widespread in consumer industries. Unemployment reached 14 percent by 1985 and showed no signs of topping off. The food-induced recession that began in 1983-4 continued through the next four years, deepening and widening rather than recovering. In an attempt to save the social security program, which would have gone bankrupt if it had continued to be indexed to inflation, the administration cut grants to all recipients and reduced yearly increments, making the cost of food all the worse for the elderly. The food stamp program was costing the U.S. $80 billion a year by 1987 and was the fastest growing segment of the budget. The deficit of $160 billion in the same year, with its accompanying 20 percent inflation, discredited the economic policies of conservative Republicans and created a clamor for an old-line liberal government.

Although the United States was benefiting from exports of expensive foodstuffs (its balance of payments showed a surplus for several years), the idea that food was a weapon for peace turned out to be false. Rather than being seen as a blessing, expensive U.S. grain was condemned as the cause of suffering, and Americans once more were blamed for what were essentially global problems. Sacked embassies, kidnapped personnel, and increased violence against Americans rendered American presence in Third World countries, both military and commercial, more problematic and risky.

Political leaders in food-dependent countries had to subsidize staple foods or face violence and insurrection. Subsidies were expensive in any form, whether by foreign loans or higher domestic taxation. With Western consumer markets in a tailspin, many Asian countries experienced their first recession since World War II. Especially hard hit were Japan, Taiwan, Korea, and Hong Kong. The lesser developed countries that had strapped themselves with unmanageable loans in the seventies, in order to finance purchases of oil, now found the added burden of expensive food more than they could bear. Loans remained unpaid. Brazil, Peru, and Indonesia failed to keep up with their interest payments on debts already several times refinanced by the International Monetary Fund. The crushing burden of expensive food and energy created political factionalism and repression. In one after another debt-ridden country, democracy gave way to dictatorship or communism. A global depression had begun.

With the strain on the banking system from defaulting Third World loans, continued double-digit inflation, ever higher deficit spending, and the realization that consumer demand was dead, certainly for the decade, perhaps forever, the stock market crumbled in 1987. Fortunes made in the early eighties, when the Dow Jones approached 2,000, disappeared overnight. Pension funds were the biggest losers of all. An increasing number of corporations suspended dividends. Savings institutions saw their deposits decrease, their loans default, and their portfolios shrink. Larger banks swallowed smaller banks and the liquidity of America and Americans came increasingly into question. Seeing that their unfunded pension liabilities had practically doubled overnight, corporations began laying off employees. Corporations that didn't or couldn't reduce staff found that these liabilities, in some cases, exceeded or equaled their net worth, in effect making them valueless. Municipalities and state governments had to reduce staff by hiring freezes and early retirement.

Despite these cost-cutting moves, defaults on bond payments swelled until the bond market was in shambles. Hardest hit were the aging industrial centers from New England to Chicago. With high unemployment and negative economic growth, many municipalities went bankrupt. States like Ohio could not cope with their Clevelands, Akrons, and Toledos all becoming insolvent at once.

During the time that food emerged as a major resource problem, energy continued to decrease in supply and rise in price. Although total worldwide demand leveled off, supplies dropped more drastically than had been anticipated. U.S. production of oil declined to 5.3 million barrels per day from 8.6 million in 1980. Cuts in production by Saudi Arabia, Kuwait, and Libya totaled another 3 million barrels per day. Some of the shortfall was made up by increased production in Indonesia and Nigeria. Some was made up by increased U.S. production of natural gas. The utilities turned increasingly to coal. But the overall effect was higher prices. By 1983 oil was $65; by 1987, $100; by 1990, $134.

When Ford, the company that had pioneered mass production, ceased manufacturing cars in 1990, pundits announced the end of the "mass" economy. A major restructuring of the economy had occurred. Because of high food and energy costs, disposable income had dropped to a level on par with the English. Economic activities that depended on excess disappeared: fast food stands, record shops, film-processing stores, boutiques, tourist businesses.

The rise in unemployment, the expense of energy, and the unavailability of credit made it both difficult and pointless for corporations to choose to invest in machines. The cost of labor had gone down in relation to capital, making it more economical for factories to use manual methods rather than automation in many cases. A century-long process of mechanization began to reverse. The high cost of transportation made regional manufacture more economical than national manufacture. Large companies lost their grip on national markets. Consumption patterns

155

changed. Purchasers made their choices with utmost caution and wariness. People wanted simple, stripped down, "no frills" products that would last. New products had to be reasonably priced and well made.

Though intended to stem profiteering in the distribution of meats, oils, staples, and gasoline, ration coupons and allocation programs created black markets instead. With food so profitable an enterprise, gardens sprang up in backyards and vacant lots. For several years canning jars were practically unobtainable. Truck farms and market gardens flourished and many of the supposedly unemployed became street vendors and middlemen in the new distribution pattern.

The psychological shock was widespread. No one had predicted the situation America found itself in by 1990. Gold and silver bugs, who had predicted collapse, saw their own investments plunge as countries liquidated metal holdings to buy food. Starting in 1987, the deflation of value in financial assets (with the exception of food-producing land) left very few sources of available capital. It was hard to get jobs, nobody was starting businesses, gas was too expensive to use for driving, food was chronically scarce, and real estate values had plunged. A walk through a suburb might reveal boarded up stores at the shopping center, grass growing through cracks in the roads, vandalized street lights, dried up lawns, and many yards torn up for gardens. Many people felt that they had worked hard for years to achieve economic goals that would insure security and relative freedom from worry. But like a bet on a wrong horse, the effort was for nought. The prospect of having to work even harder just to dig out from under proved overwhelming to many professionals.

America no longer seemed to be America. The ambience, the feel of the city streets was more like Europe in the late forties. For many the quiet was unsettling. Except in the open-air markets, noise levels dropped. More people were sitting on stoops, in parks, on benches. Since unemployed parents had no need of day-care centers, children were back on the streets. Men spent more time with their children. Large armies of male stockbrokers, lawyers, and middle managers found themselves out of work. Wives with humbler jobs became family breadwinners, while their once highly paid husbands gradually lowered their expectations for employment and began to learn new skills — employable skills.

The high cost of transportation meant that people could not freely travel. With people remaining close to home most of the time, their communities and jobs ranked as their highest priorities. Communities organized themselves around the three main problems: food, energy, and the economy. Municipalities realized that the creation of local sources of energy would strengthen their economies, save money, increase tax revenue, and help local industry. As oil crossed the $100 per barrel barrier, wind, photovoltaic, and solar all became economical. Rarely would you walk into a building that was heated over sixty degrees. People walked to town, rode buses, bicycled, or thumbed rides. Jitneys multiplied in big cities. Suburbs formed intricate carpool networks. Cars moved more slowly.

The change in living habits by the nineties was considerable. Cars traveled an average of 3,000 miles per year unless owned and used by a group. Energy consumption had been reduced nationwide by 25 percent and was dropping. Dried foods were plentiful. Basic produce was obtainable in season. Beyond that, depending on time and locale, food was not always available. Brand name proliferation ceased. Generic items stocked by retailing chains accounted for 70 percent of the average market basket. Magazines and newsletters circulated with the sole purpose of putting consumers in touch with growers. Families would pool money, take a station wagon or pickup to upper New York State from Manhattan, and come back with cheese, fowl, flour, bacon, apples, and honey. Farmers in North Dakota would ship their wheat directly to bigger buying clubs, usually by rail. The commonality of needs made for tighter neighborhoods and towns.

As usual, the candidates who ran for office in 1992 failed to comprehend the mood of the electorate. Conservatives ran as liberals, and Democrats sounded like socialists. You couldn't be populist enough, a complete philosophical reversal of the laissez-faire individualism that had characterized the eighties. Despite the Democratic sweep, the vote was one of anger and resentment, not endorsement. The credibility of effective government action had been shattered. Most families were having to scramble to keep their kids fed, their checking accounts solvent, and their houses away from creditors.

Despite adaptive steps taken by individuals and groups in response to new conditions, the succession of economic crises compounded the already severe psychological crises. Charitable groups set up intervention and counseling centers to deal with the enormous increase in child abuse, battered wives, alcoholism, and teen-age crime. Having begun the decade with mortgages and consumer debt, many families went bankrupt. Some had continued to borrow more deeply in hopes that the economy would turn around or that inflation would reduce their debt in real dollars. Stories abounded of successful professionals who had gone from prosperity to penury within a year. Families that belonged to churches and other extended social groups fared better, but the toll on the American family was grave.

Overnight, it seemed as if everyone's hair had turned grayer. Some looked as though they had a bad hangover. For others it was an awakening. Those who had been living simply for many years fared the best. Those who had plodded along free of debt in the eighties found themselves less affected. Partly because of the blow to expectations and pride, many men seemed to sulk and only half-heartedly participate in the new social configurations. Women thrived as they successfully competed for mayoralties, governorships, and senate seats. People were less interested in candidates' "answers," more impressed by their true concern. In expressing and in demonstrating concern, women appeared superior to male candidates. During the decade, the only significant national and international movement was the continued proliferation and growth of the women's movement. The near collapse of so many male-dominated institutions created a vacuum that women easily and energetically filled. With fewer dogmas to defend, women proved freer and more adaptive in mind and spirit. While politics went on under traditional Republican and Democratic guise, this did not conceal a real shift in power from men to women.

The challenge that faced all leaders was how to solve problems with a depleted tax base. The most pressing problems were city services: garbage, libraries, lighting, crime, and sewage. The town hall meetings that quickly emerged to solve the problems often seemed to breed contention; but in the end, the fact remained that the cities got along nearly as well with less money as they had with more. As money was withdrawn from the complex systems that had come to run people's lives, the only way the systems could function was with more human attention. Neighbors swept their own streets and collected refuse in recyclable containers. Presorting garbage and lowered consumption of throwaways reduced solid waste by 80 percent. Cooperatives proliferated: child-care, food distribution, auto repair, nurseries, and housing. Both men and women trained as volunteers to augment professional firefighters. Paramedical services sprouted up so that medical emergencies and routine health care could be administered locally. Neighbors patrolled streets at night to supplement police services.

People came to value good friends and neighbors more highly than money. If you wanted something done that was more than you alone could or wanted to do — a drainage ditch, a new roof, a windmill — you took it to the neighborhood instead of to professionals. Services were largely traded, and elaborate mechanisms emerged to keep tabs on who owed what to whom. People saved their cash for durables, gas, rent, and food. The strengthened interconnectedness of neighborhoods proved a strong deterrent to anti-social behavior including crime. Selfishness did not work under so many watchful eyes. Lone wolves went broke. As welfare disappeared due to shortages of funds, people relied upon each other for help formerly granted by government. Rugged individualism stuck out rather awkwardly, and self-sufficiency was of value to the group only if it allowed greater participation in the group.

Those who had stored guns, food, precious metals, medicines, and toilet paper as a means of surviving appeared selfish and were treated with suspicion. Such Dickensian paranoia seemed strangely out of touch with reality, because, while the daily news was bad indeed, an entirely altered social structure was emerging. Hoarders had money to be sure, but they were left with nothing at all to do but slowly spend it as needs arose. The people who had gained from the long economic contraction were those with useful skills, goodwill, and a willingness to help others. Anyone who could call a good square dance at night and weld a cracked undercarriage during the day was a person whose stock rose measurably in any community. Such people lost nothing.

The politics of the late eighties and early nineties were extremely diverse. One state after another, one county after another, woke up to the fact that directions were no longer emanating from Washington. In most areas the change prompted the emergence of a new sense of responsibility. It was as if bands of over-protected adolescents had suddenly grown into adulthood. People acknowledged their capacities to take care of themselves and those immediately around them.

The debates that had been recorded over two centuries ago in the Federalist Papers were being re-enacted in at least a dozen different "nations," each the size of the original experiment. Just as the American Revolution had been fought for the sake of independence from a distant and seemingly indifferent agency of taxation, so the new regionalism was an expression of autonomy and independence from a Washington bureaucracy perceived as corrupt, ineffectual, and far too greedy for taxation without adequate or appropriate representation. The rise of interest groups in the sixties and seventies had begun to speak to the problem. In a declining industrial economy no longer agriculturally based, ties to the land — to strictly geographical representation — proved inappropriate. Upwardly mobile electronics engineers, gay rights activists, advocates of the ERA, and minority groups drew support from widely distributed constituencies. Yet the new ties to widely distributed interest groups proved just as inappropriate to the new bio-regional politics of the nineties. Geographical location — now by region rather than by private acreage — became politically significant once again. National interest groups succeeded only in paralyzing Washington rather than reforming it.

A more radical reform than interest group politics, the new quest for regional independence revolved around a need to make room for a plurality of belief systems. In the eighteenth century, the desire for religious freedom had motivated many to seek out new lives in the more tolerant New World. Two centuries later, political beliefs had largely replaced religious beliefs in the role of providing the basic principles guiding social interactions. Where theological disputes had once elicited the strongest passions and the cruelest punishments, now political debate had taken over a similar role. So it was natural that the new struggles for independence would take the form of political rather than religious pluralism. Political tolerance replaced religious tolerance as the dominant principle. In place of the freedom to worship as one pleased, the new American Revolution promoted the right to politicize as one pleased.

Politically, the options were endless. In the Southwest, politics soon reverted to the kind of feudalism that had characterized much of the area well into the twentieth century. A landed aristocracy exercised autocratic rule over a peasantry consisting largely of illegal aliens from Mexico. The urban Northeast became the Great Britain of the new order. Massive defaults by Third World countries delivered blows to the financial community that were as damaging to the preeminence of the Northeast as the wars of independence had been to British colonial rule. An injured nobility and a dissatisfied populace then tore at each other in a series of intense parliamentary battles; the outcome was a maze of statutes and administrative decisions virtually designed to accelerate the "English disease" — declining productivity.

Rural New England was quite another story. Ingenuity, deep roots, and a stubborn insistence on the viability of old American values gave rise to networks of thriving communities where decaying mill towns had stood decades earlier. Vermont, New Hampshire, and western Massachusetts solved their energy problems with diverse combinations of wood, hydroelectric, wind, and solar power. Food and dairy cooperatives flourished. Old mills that had been empty for decades were filled by groups of small manufacturing companies that produced goods mostly for regional consumption, thereby decreasing the deficit in the area's traditionally poor balance of payments with the rest of the country. Products like toothpaste and soap, for which approximately 20 percent of the counter price had gone to advertising and transportation from large, brand-name factories situated mostly in the South, were now produced locally for lower cost and with higher employment.

California, always big enough to be its own country, continued on its several courses. It continued to be America's import-export agent for the economy of the Pacific Basin and still produced a large amount of food. The entertainment industry suffered losses as the networks and studios of Hollywood continued to lose market shares to entertainment centers that were ever more regional. But in Northern California the microelectronics industry survived. Since most of the systems of the seventies remained on go, the state as a whole changed less than the country. California, the country's cutting edge during the sixties and seventies, became by the nineties a cultural museum of a former era.

Among the most politically and culturally independent of the several regions was the OPEC-like coalition of the sparsely populated, energy-rich Western states. Wyoming, with its fiercely independent tradition for protecting its wilderness from outsiders, became the Iran of the new intranational politics. By imposing prohibitive taxes on corporations that owned some of the mineral rights to vast deposits of oil shale there, the government eventually forced sales of the rights back to the State

Mineral Authority. Then the prices began to rise. Utah played more of a Saudi Arabian game, supplying vast quantities of coal at relatively reasonable prices.

The new pluralism extended beyond energy systems and politics to culture and religion. The alternatives had become sharper: either you tried to play the old game in which the stakes were ever higher, or you started a new league. There were models aplenty by the late eighties. But precisely in their plurality, diverse communities made it clear that there was not just one right way to live a human life, not just one solution to the social problem. Rather it was a matter of group efforts at creativity. Each group had to find its own particular niche in the cultural ecology. There could be only so many communities oriented around computers in a given county, and only so many farms to feed the computer repair specialists and other professionals and paraprofessionals.

As we now see, the real success of these new communities lay in their refusals to become ghettoized. Specialization and division of labor were no longer purchased at the price of all-consuming professionalism. Different communities had different characters, different specialties, but each community made a real effort at a limited self-sufficiency.

Excellence, quality, and craft were highly valued, but the mock heroics of self-sacrifice in the service of narrow expertise were recognized as ultimately counterproductive. Part of the role of communities of common interest came to be the reinforcement of personal breadth rather than that imitation of depth that earlier decades had sought in specialization.

The sixties and seventies had thrown professionals together in competitive guilds to see who would work the hardest to learn one thing well. The norms and ideals that took root in the eighties and nineties stressed the need for a full humanity as the final important ingredient in everyone's training. Following the debacles perpetrated by narrowminded experts just doing their jobs, most of the new pros refused to put on the official uniforms of their forebears. White coats disappeared from the lab and pin stripe suits went to the back of the closet. New codes of conviviality substituted for the uniforms that had come to conceal more than they revealed about the human beings beneath them.

Some still engage in scholarship and train others to do likewise. But scholarship is no longer the measure by which most learning is judged. Rather than serving as a set of hurdles through which all must pass if they are to gain the credentials to perform in other professions, scholarship is now the calling of a few dedicated intellectuals who pursue it more out of passion than from a sense of scrupulous obligation.

Just as each person aspired to the cultivation of many talents, so each locale became a microcosm of a complete and sustainable society. The specialization of terrain went the way of the specialization of the human spirit. Light industry and intensive gardening infiltrated the suburbs. Many of the old industrial parks were inhabited by human beings who reclaimed the land that had been dedicated to cars. The vast parking lots that surrounded many of the old factories eventually housed more workers than the number that had parked their cars in the same space decades earlier. The integration of health-care services and schools in those communities made for a degree of self-sufficiency that had been unknown.

Entertainment and sports took on a degree of importance they had not had before. There, too, the cult of the experts, the superstars, gave way to the cultivation of everyone's skills. With the return of an appreciation for discipline among more than just a few fanatics, many people practiced arts and skills for which they were richly rewarded in their own communities, whether or not they were elevated to stardom and dragged out on tour. Since passive spectatorship suffered ever decreasing regard, and active participation ever higher respect, professional sports and high-priced concerts came in for contempt. Live music returned to living rooms. Sales in softballs soared.

During the nineties, the Oriental religions that had earlier been exotic imports finally took root. The transplants took. They looked different when grown upon American soil, but after a generation or two, hybridization was well on its way. Perhaps most important of all, independent of the specific doctrinal contents of the imports, children would no longer grow up hearing only about the God of Abraham. The One God of the Catholics and the Protestants and the Jews was suddenly, and for the children quite satisfactorily, just one among several gods: Shiva and Krishna and Brahma and so on. Those who were already adults when the imports first arrived continued to believe that they worshipped the one true lord. But the presence of other religions on their very own shores, the frequent references in their children's conversations, constituted no real offense to their monotheistic faith. For the children, on the other hand, polytheism was the new order of the day; not the polytheism of the Greeks or the Hindus, but the polytheism of America at the close of the twentieth century. Like ancient Greece, North America had become overrun with preachers of many faiths.

The change in the U.S.'s world role was as dramatic as the change in its internal structure. Good fortune more than anything else kept the U.S. and U.S.S.R. out of a direct confrontation. Both "superpowers" engaged in marginally successful military adventures — the Philippines for the U.S. and Yugoslavia for the U.S.S.R. But each had become less a superpower by the nineties. Those climbing the development ladder via a capitalist route took as their models Japan, Taiwan, Germany, and France rather than any of the English-speaking nations. The evidence of a stodgy economy, a repressive bureaucracy, and an adventurist military eroded the U.S.S.R.'s leadership role. China, Tanzania, Sweden, Romania, and Sri Lanka led the socialist world.

While several developmental paths persist — from socialist Sri Lanka to an increasingly prosperous and repressive Brazil — America is still emulated by others. The rapid change in the U.S. has not gone unnoticed. The seeming resilience of the world's richest country has increased its respect in the eyes of many. Whatever the gross inequities or faults of America, it seems in the eyes of the world as preeminent as ever. The economic shocks of the eighties left no nation untouched, but where many succumbed to cumbersome administrative answers to complex geopolitical problems, the United States seems to crackle with a kind of excitement that others envy. It is a grassroots movement, a change in the American mood. The old individualism has run its course. One by one individuals discover their common collectivity in the obvious impossibility of their increasing isolation. America has not survived. It has revived.

The title Living Within Our Means implies a world in which people are well adapted to their circumstance. But as in Beginnings of Sorrow, the means have been drastically reduced. Living within them is hardly a choice, it is a painful necessity born of reality. The industrial paradigm runs smack against the declining carrying capacity of the earth. The new but practical economic model stresses real personal satisfaction rather than personal consumption. Emerson's ideal of "plain living and high thinking" taps deeply into strong American values and abilities of self-sufficiency and neighborliness. We make the best of what is bad because we are in fact prepared, because we consistently opt for responsibility, and because we choose to stay together as a people, as a society, and as a country. We discover strengths that had long been forgotten in the relative ease of contemporary life.

Table 15
Statistics: Living Within Our Means

	1980	2000
World Population (in millions)	4,500	6,300
U.S. Population (in millions)	226	268
World GNP (in billions)	7,000	10,000
U.S. GNP (in billions)	2,600	2,170
U.S. Per Capita Disposable Income	8,100	5,340
U.S. Per Capita Consumption Expenditures	7,400	5,050
Average World Energy Prices ($/bbl crude)	35	100
Energy Consumption (quads)	78	70
Energy Supply by Source (quads)		
Domestic Oil	20	15
Imported Oil	15	7
Shale Oil	0	0
Natural Gas	20	14
Coal	17	18
Conventional Nuclear	3	3
Nuclear Breeder	0	0
Solar, Hydropower, and Other	3	13
Percentage of Income Spent On		
Housing	21	25
Food	21	34
Clothing	8	11
Medical Care	10	7
Transportation	15	17

Note: 1 quad = 10^{15} Btu/yr; all dollar figures are in 1980 dollars.

Table 16
Trends: Living Within Our Means

*Countries growing economically: ***

Australia	China
Canada	Brazil
Norway	South Africa

*Countries contracting economically: ****

Japan	Egypt
Indonesia	Iran
United Kingdon	Mexico

Occupations which are rapidly growing in demand:

Co-op managers	Musical instrument makers
Local politicians	Seamstresses
Small businesses	Farmers
Craftspersons	Recycling
Midwifery	Waste treatment

Occupations which are shrinking in demand:

Lawyers	Advertising
Accountants	University professors
Middle managers	Nuclear engineering
Hollywood producers	

Businesses which are growing:

Recycling	Handtools
Repair	Farming
Local entertainment	Coal

Businesses which are contracting:

Airlines	Processed food
Broadcast TV	Consumer luxury goods
Banking .	Resorts
Fast food	

*Top 10 percent in growth of GNP 1995-2000
**Bottom 5 percent in growth of GNP 1995-2000

PART THREE
TOWARD A
VOLUNTARY
HISTORY

THE INTENT OF THE SCENARIOS is to heighten our sensitivity to the consequences of current choices, not to foretell the inevitable or enchant us with the most desirable future. As a mental exercise, they should increase our agility in choosing and understanding our possibilities and adapting to our realities. They give us a sense of the potential interplay of forces, events, and human choices that shape the future. What lessons can we learn from them?

The Official Future extends the trends and aspirations of the fifties and early sixties. For that reason it remains a desirable future for many Americans whose values were formed during those decades. But the clash of that image against the realities of the seventies and eighties renders the Official Future a less than likely scenario. Mature Calm does not demand all the good breaks from a benign set of circumstances as the Official Future does. But Mature Calm does depend on a degree of social cohesion that is unlikely in our highly fragmented society. The Center Holds may be attractive to some, but it suggests calling off the American experiment in human freedom. Periods of crisis and distress color the other four scenarios. Living Within Our Means and Apocalyptic Transformation achieve something close to happy endings, at least from some contemporary perspectives.

But it is difficult to regard as desirable any scenarios that begin with such dark days. Furthermore, from such problematic beginnings, Chronic Breakdown and Beginnings of Sorrow appear to be at least as likely if not more likely outcomes.

In short, if we fail to take charge of our destiny, we may find that the most desirable futures are least likely, while the most likely are the least desirable.

The scenarios set us a problem. A healthy economy seems to be necessary to insure peace, freedom, and a sense of hope about the future. But the inertia of history deeds us a situation in which the health of the economy depends on an energy system so fragile its survival may take us to war on the one hand, or toward the authoritarian management of economic and natural resources on the other. Or both.

In this concluding section we tackle the interplay of energy, national security, the economy, and finally, our basic values. As the diagram on page 29 and the scenarios show, the future cleaves not only on the external vicissitudes of a world in transition, but also on the personal values upheld by America's inhabitants. While not ignoring the very real problems and challenges that confront us, we nevertheless assert that the problems will be approached in very different ways depending upon the values we bring to bear on the problems as we perceive them.

Aside from the events and characters, the major fiction of the scenarios is their hindsight. In this final section, we reverse the perspective and look ahead. Having no wish to compete with alarmists or doomsayers, we do not identify any single issue as the crisis for which we must drop everything else to free our hands for some singular solution. There is, rather, a need to describe an ethical and perceptual stance that does quite the opposite, a stance that positions us as a nation for a future that none of us can possibly know or predict. The future we eventually inhabit will doubtless contain elements from several if not all of the preceding scenarios. Just as the scenarios will mix in a melange too rich for any single story, so too the central issues of energy, national security, economics, and values mix in a tangled web of interdependence. Having explored in narrative hindsight the interconnections of issues to generate different scenarios, we now explore those same interconnections with analytic foresight to more directly address the problems posed by the consequences observed in the scenarios. Problem-solving, not prediction, is the ultimate purpose of the exercise of scenario building. Having seen, in however fictional a form, the probable consequences of certain decisions, we now have an opportunity to avert some of those less desirable consequences — if only we comprehend the interrelationships between issues and the role of present choices in determining future outcomes.

Chapter X

Energy

TWO DISTINCT ENERGY CRISES demand consideration, since both will have a profound effect on the politics, productivity, and well-being of Americans. The first is the short-term crisis of Western dependency on imported oil from the unstable Persian Gulf countries; the second crisis is of a longer term and involves the transition toward renewable sources of energy such as solar and bio-mass. Both crises consist of two parts: the supply of energy available for use, and the demand for energy likely to exist.

The crisis of Western dependency is a result of two forces. The first is profligate consumption. Although the United States has recently reduced its overall oil consumption, it continues to burn up 32 percent of the world's production, about 10,000 gallons per second, despite the fact that its population and total proven reserves amount to less than 5 percent of the world's total. Furthermore, the total production from those reserves is falling off every year, despite enhanced recovery techniques, decontrol of wellhead prices, and renewed exploration. It is doubtful, even given a national emergency, that national production could exceed greatly the 8 million barrels per day currently produced, an amount that meets slightly more than half of our oil needs.

The second force at work in the short term is the fact that oil is not equally distributed around the world. Of the remaining reserves, approximately 55 percent lie beneath the countries immediately surrounding the Persian Gulf, 15 percent is controlled by other OPEC nations, and another 16 percent is within communist countries, primarily the Soviet Union. In 1970 only 6 percent of the oil in non-communist countries was owned by producer countries; 94 percent was owned by oil companies. By 1979 producer countries had gained 55 percent ownership to the oil companies' 45 percent. Because the price of a barrel of oil does not depend on extraction costs within the United States but on bidding in the international market, the critical oil that governs the behavior of the international market is the politically and economically volatile oil that flows from the Middle East. The greater part of the 50 percent rise in oil prices from 1979 until early 1981 was due entirely to the wars within and between two of the Middle Eastern countries: Iran and Iraq. Thus, the sensitivity of world markets to political and cultural dramas played out in that part of the world becomes even more acute as time goes on.

These two forces must deal with the unique history of that region of the world where religious, tradition-bound societies strain under a massive infusion of wealth and its corresponding pressure for modernization. Until 1973, when the nations of the Persian Gulf sold as much oil as the world wanted to buy, supply was limited only by the ability to expand capacity. Since 1973, when the OPEC nations formed a cartel to maximize their oil income, there has been a shift in wealth from the oil-consuming nations to the oil-producing nations. This wealth has spurred large and rapid programs of modernization throughout the Persian Gulf, and in turn has introduced a new and formidable factor into the oil-exporting policies of the Persian Gulf nations. Governments of the oil nations, as they continue to receive massive amounts of foreign currency, have only two choices in disbursing it. They can spend it on programs of modernization, including new schools, cities, ports, and factories. But, as witnessed in Iran, such rapid change carries with it the threat of internal revolution from the avidly conservative, religious traditionalists so prevalent in the Persian Gulf nations. Thoughts of houses renting for $8,000 per month in Riyadh, of disabled Mercedes Benzs abandoned in the desert because their owners would rather buy new ones than find the cause of the troubles, of the breakdown of patriarchal forms of control endemic to Islamic beliefs — these thoughts do not make the religiously fervent desirous of selling more oil. The losses outweigh the gains in a culture that is on the whole nonmaterialistic. The essentially religious nature of the Iranian revolution is not so much anti-American as it is pro-traditional Islamic values. Anti-American-ism stems from America's role as a symbol of the untried, the untested and the new, as well as our association with pro-develop-ment but sometimes repressive regimes. Simply speaking, Islam is a highly fundamentalist religion that does not mix easily with the Western values that follow dollars into Islamic countries.

Once the governments of the oil-producing Persian Gulf nations reach the culturally imposed upper limit of domestic spending, money can be disbursed by loaning, depositing, or investing it back into the Western countries from whence it came. But if too much of a country's wealth returns to Western hands, and its leaders are seen as being too pro-Western (the Shah, the Saudi royal family), then Arab rulers face charges from dissident fundamentalists that the country's wealth is "out" of the country, and can either be seized by Western countries as the United States seized Iranian assets, or taken by the leader(s) of the country as did the Shah. The magnitude of the problem should not be underestimated. Spending money is a "problem" few face; thus it carries a fantasy quality rather than a problematic one. Never-theless, the dilemma is a grave one with OPEC surpluses in 1980 exceeding $100 billion. By 1990 surpluses could approach $350 billion per year. Lending the money to poorer Third World countries to help them finance their escalating oil bills has become equally problematic since their debts already exceed $400 billion. Many countries are already borrowing just to make interest payments on old debts. Whether the oil-producing countries keep their money at home for modernization or try to recycle it abroad, rightists see their heritage in jeopardy and leftists see their country's wealth misappropriated.

Many of the OPEC nations may already be reaching the limits

of their ability to absorb Western currency. This problem is being played out in a decade when the United States and probably the Soviet Union will have to import more oil than at present. There is no reason to believe that oil consumption in Japan, Germany, France, Brazil, Korea, and other countries will decrease dramatically either. If the short-term demand for energy rises and there is not an increased supply, the price of oil will naturally go up. If the price goes up and sales are kept constant, these countries will have even more income to contend with. Since they cannot absorb more money, they may cut supply. The bidding for the remaining oil will intensify and the price will go up further. This is the reverse of the usual supply-and-demand relationship. Usually, when increased demand drives prices higher, producers increase supplies to cash in on the combination of high demand and high prices. But this case — demand goes up, price goes up, but supply goes down — is an economic anomaly.

A higher oil price will mean that oil now locked in this country will begin to flow. It costs money to get oil. Some oil is cheaper to get than other oil. Most of the oil we now use is very cheap — a few cents a barrel for extraction costs. Some oil is very expensive to get because it is too thick or too thin, too far under water or too deep underground. Although the higher price for oil will mean renewed exploration and development of domestic oil, most of the economically accessible oil in the United States has been tapped and exploited. What remains will be costly to develop and slow to bring on stream, meaning that total U.S. production is unlikely to rise. It will merely decline more slowly.

The fundamental, short-term problem is that over the next five to ten years — short of a severe economic recession — the industrialized world will not restrain its demand for oil enough to avoid upward pressure on prices. The consequence of that upward pressure on price, downward pressure on supply, and continued demand by the industrialized world could be hyperinflation, deflation and depression, or the likelihood of war. Or possibly all three.

What about our long-term prospects? Some time in the

not-too-distant future, we are going to have to begin to make a transition from burning fossil fuels to other sources of energy — not only because of scarcity. Fossil fuels refined as lubricants, synthetics, and plastics have no substitute and are therefore exceptionally useful materials. The less we burn, the more remains available for these uses. Just as important, burning fossil fuels produces excessive carbon dioxide. We are already experiencing a massive build-up of carbon dioxide in the atmosphere from the worldwide combination of combustion and deforestation, and no one as yet knows the implications of such a change of the earth's atmosphere by human intervention. Three main theories regarding this phenomenon conflict with each other, but none bode well so it may not matter who is right. One argues that the earth will experience a greenhouse effect which will melt the polar ice caps and raise the ocean level 20 to 25 feet. A second theory foresees rapid glaciation. A third suggests that the warming trend of carbon dioxide build-up will conflict with a long-term cooling trend and cause erratic, turbulent, and highly volatile climatic patterns. In all three scenarios, food and agriculture will be adversely affected. Whatever the effects, they will be intensified by the continued production of carbon dioxide.

Both the long-term and short-term energy crises are rendered more complex by two additional factors. First, we may use many different forms of energy, and although each form is reducible to a mathematical equivalency in BTUs, the different forms are not easily substitutable for each other. We use oil for transportation, electricity, and heat; coal for electricity, heat, and steam; gas for heating and cooking; and electricity for lighting, motors, and appliances. But we cannot run planes on electricity, cars on coal, stoves on synfuels, or motors on firewood. Laying out an energy supply picture is thus more than counting barrels and thermal units. It involves having the right form of energy at the right place, which reduces the overall utility of all energy supplies to the specific work a specific source can perform.

Another complicating factor affecting our choices among energy systems derives from the fact that our choices in part determine what kind of society we will have. In *Soft Energy Paths,* Amory Lovins argues that a future that relies on increasingly capital-intensive and complex sources of energy — for example, nuclear, oil, and fusion — will necessitate a corresponding centralization of power in society and lead to diminished overall freedom and increased authoritarianism. Conversely, a society that practices increased conservation while developing an array of renewable sources of energy will lead to a decentralized, freer culture that will not need to be as externally warlike. The choice among energy systems, then, may not merely determine how our toast is toasted or what kind of hardware we are building; that choice determines the kind of society we are building as well.

To summarize this treatment of the short-term and long-term energy crises: the industrialized world is currently caught in the vise of an economic anomaly known as a backward-sloping supply curve created by heavy dependency on undependable suppliers who may not be able to absorb expanding amounts of U.S. dollars. In the long term, we must reduce consumption of fossil fuels because of scarcity, lack of substitutes, and because their combustion creates a carbon dioxide problem. In both short and long terms, we need not just energy, but particular forms of energy.

To construct a realistic energy policy, we have to consider what contributions various potential energy supplies might make over what period of time, and what effects various measures to reduce demand might have over what period of time. Between now and 1985, there is very little we can do to voluntarily control the situation. On the supply side, it is theoretically possible to increase imports of oil and to slow the decrease of domestic oil production. But no significant quantities of any other major energy source can come on line before 1985. On the demand side, higher prices will generally lead more people to be more efficient in their use of energy.

If we cannot increase domestic production of oil and we cannot increase imports, what can we do? Coal is one answer, but coal has its problems. We are not geared up to produce as much coal as we need. We do not have the mining rigs, the coal cars, the railways or the pipelines that a shift toward coal would require. The costs will run into the many billions. Environmental questions about the mining and burning of coal cannot easily be dismissed.

Even if coal could be produced in large quantities almost overnight, that would not solve our problem. Our system is now geared to oil and gas. We still need liquid and gaseous fuels. The technology for making oil and gas from coal exists. However, the ability to produce large quantities of either synthetic oil or synthetic gas has not yet been demonstrated. Environmental questions have yet to be addressed. Most of the processes use a great deal of water, as does the technology for making oil from shale rock. However, the coal and the shale are in the arid high plains and Rocky Mountain states, such as Montana, Wyoming, and Colorado, where the battle lines on access to water and land are already being drawn. Shale oil in western Colorado may mean an end to irrigated farming in eastern Colorado.

If nuclear power were safe and economical it might ease our problem. Rather than being solved, the problems of nuclear power are mounting. Under duress we might decide to build many more new nuclear plants. Even if all the regulations were waived it would still take four or five years to build a number of plants. With proper safeguards the process would take a decade or more. We might become dependent on imported uranium instead of imported oil.

Solar technologies for space and hot water heating, as well as silicon cells for converting sunlight to electricity, look very promising. The eighties should find wide application of solar technology. The Atlantic Richfield Company (ARCO) plans to market a new roofing tile that contains solar cells, so that every home becomes a power station, perhaps generating enough to sell some electricity back to the utilities. But a solar industry does not exist today and will take some time to create.

Much is often made of hoped-for breakthroughs, especially in technology. Most attention focuses on fusion power — the energy

179

released by the fusion of hydrogen atoms to form helium at temperatures in the millions of degrees. Fusion may someday be a practical energy source. But in any practical form and useful quantities, fusion power is three or more decades off. Very cheap solar electric cells, solar power satellites, ocean thermal — exotically named and potentially very useful energy sources — all will take time and will be costly in the short run.

Perhaps we'll discover more resources. One intriguing possibility is the theory that there may be much more natural gas buried at very deep levels in the earth. The theory argues that natural gas comes not only from the decay of ancient biological matter, but from deep and even more ancient geologic processes as well. A great deal more research is needed to verify the theory, but if it is correct, then the long-term energy picture would change radically. For a very long time to come, perhaps many centuries, nearly everyone could have access to a widely useful, nearly universal fuel that burns without pollution, but at a high cost. Because it lies so deep, extraction would be very expensive. We would have abundance but it would have to be an efficient abundance. The theory, however, is treated skeptically by many experts. It will take years before even the theory is proven right or wrong.

A radical change in behavior might offer another kind of breakthrough. Perhaps a large enough number of people are voluntarily shifting their behavior to consume less. Duane Elgin's book *Voluntary Simplicity* and Mark Markley's *Changing Images of Man* provide evidence of such a value shift. Surveys of consumer attitudes and behaviors conducted by SRI's Values and Lifestyles Program show that the fastest growing group of consumers are those whose values lead them toward reduced levels of consumption. We believe that in the long run a shift in this direction is very possible, even likely, out of both necessity and desire. But rapid, radical change of behavior in a group of people large enough to have a great impact can only occur as the outcome of fairly traumatic events. Living Within Our Means is a scenario based on that assumption. The outcome of such trauma is just as likely to result in scenarios like the Center Holds, Beginnings of Sorrow, or Chronic Breakdown.

Whether the breakthrough is in technology, resources, or behavior does not matter. It seems imprudent and foolish to bet the future on breakthroughs. If they come, we may be better off for them, but none of the breakthroughs can make much difference in the short run. To create an energy system that requires a future breakthrough for its continuity tends to lead to a highly constrained future. Thus, concentrating on breakthroughs as the primary direction of research and development seems to be a diversion from more potentially useful work on such things as industrial efficiency, coal technology, and conservation.

Given the current range of options combined with the potential problems attached to each, the most important criterion in making our individual and collective energy decisions is the question of preserving options. In ignoring our wasteful consumption in order to preserve our sense of prosperity, we have waited much too long to make the decisions that would lead us to viable energy alternatives — and so have increased our insecurity. Theoretically, we could have started to concentrate our research and funding on solar energy at the same time we chose nuclear. The amount of money spent on nuclear energy to date would insulate and solar heat over 60 percent of the homes in America, saving yearly more than all of the electricity generated by nuclear power plants. Similarly, the 1973 oil embargo served ample warning to America that its consumption of energy would have to change. But no meaningful energy program has been developed during those years, and certainly there has been no comprehensive national effort toward conservation. By forestalling meaningful action, we have closed off options that were formerly available. The options that are now available to us have been reduced to only a few, so one crucial criterion for choosing should be whether or not a given choice will preserve what options remain.

The most fundamental action we can take to preserve our future options is to reduce demand by improving the efficiency of our energy use. This first-order conservation, as we call it, can be achieved by higher energy prices resulting from the recent decontrol of oil prices, and by such measures as tax incentives for home insulation and for early rapid replacement of inefficient industrial equipment. By first-order conservation methods we can reduce energy use by one-third. Between 1982 and 1986, it will be possible to realize almost half of those gains. Equally impressive gains come from what we call second-order conservation: changed patterns of production and consumption stressing durability, quality of design, and the efficient use of energy and raw materials. Every time we make and buy a product, we are purchasing a certain amount of embodied energy consisting of the energy required to make the product, to transport the raw materials, to get the workers to the factory, to distribute, advertise, and sell the product.

Energy-driven inflation has taught us that it is cheaper to buy something once than twice, for every time we go back out in the market, inflation has made the price higher. Figuring rightly that higher priced, durable items are less expensive over the long run than repeated purchases of cheaper goods, consumers will buy items that will last longer. Such products need to be remanufactured less frequently, require fewer repairs, and over their lives consume less energy and resources. They are more expensive at the time of purchase but over their life cycles generally cost less. Producers will resist making such products until users demand them. For the user, second-order conservation does not mean a lower standard of living in real terms, but it does require a different standard of living — a change from extravagant to conservative, from inefficient to frugal, from fashionable to durable. A shift to second-order conservation takes a long time, at least a decade to take root and many more to develop. Nevertheless, meaningful gains amounting to half the gains achieved by first-order conservation could be accomplished by 1985. Thus an overall 25 percent reduction in energy demand could be accomplished in five years. This could cut our oil imports, reduce pressure on demand, ease prices, and ultimately relax international tension.

By 1990, small but significant increases in both orders of conservation could decrease overall demand by one-third. By that time conversion to coal could free up some additional amounts of oil for transportation. Solar energy could be making significant contributions in hot water heating, space heating, and in electric generation. By the mid-nineties, in addition to the previous options, there will probably be significant amounts of synthetic fuels from shale and coal. At the same time other forms of renewable energy — wind and biomass — could be making major contributions to the energy supply.

The choice then comes down to this. If we choose not to control demand — that is, not to exercise a maximum level of efficiency improvements, not to pursue first-order conservation and second-order conservation, not to make some changes in the way we live — then demand will rise. Then we will have to pursue *all* supply options as hard as we can and as fast as we can: domestic oil, coal, synthetics, nuclear, and solar. On the other hand we can elect to control demand, moderate the amount of energy we choose to use, pursue efficiency — first-order and second-order conservation — as rapidly as we are able. Then we will be able to choose among energy supply options. We will not have to pursue all energy sources as hard or as rapidly as if the demand were uncontrolled. More important, we will be less vulnerable to supply disruptions and international tensions.

The power to effect changes in energy usage rests primarily with individuals. In a democratic society where freedom is broadly distributive, so is responsibility — the ability to respond. New power plants cannot and need not be financed if data show no growth in consumption. Already nuclear plants have been tabled as a result of the rapid changes in domestic electrical usage. We have thought of ourselves as insatiable so long that we now have a fun-house mirror image of ourselves swelling at the sides with past excesses. The Democrat-controlled houses of Congress decided after the 1973 energy crisis that Americans would not cut back on gasoline consumption even if the price went up — the inelastic demand fallacy — and decided forthwith to keep the lid on domestic oil prices as a way of insulating Americans from inflation and unnecessarily high costs. Therefore, with inflation, the real cost of energy actually declined from 1974 to 1978. The price increases in world oil markets were never fully experienced by Americans until the 1979 Iranian crisis, at which point demand went down sharply and has stayed down. Prior to that, the relatively low prices of gasoline kept demand for big cars high and, despite the mandated increases in mileage per gallon required by the same Congress for domestically produced automobiles, Americans wanted the bigger cars. This confusing message to the automobile industry, on top of the increasing numbers of foreign imports, has much to do with the Chrysler Corporation debacle. If the battle to overcome the energy crises could be compared to a football game, the years between 1973 and 1980 would be roughly comparable to fumbling on our own two-yard line.

Consider a newer, more complementary role between individuals and their government that may be an easier role for both. To harken again back to the seventies, the decision to control gasoline prices and maintain artificially low ceilings produced as a direct result big cars with poor mileage ratings. This rolling stock, totaling millions of automobiles, is far from obsolete. It is being traded in by the more affluent and financially nimble classes for small imported cars, and the big cars, no longer in demand, are available for low prices. Who is buying them? The poor, of course. Our effort to help the poor by controlling gas prices backfired. Now that gas prices are high and rising fast, the poor are getting 9 mpg instead of a possible 30 mpg. The less affluent simply cannot afford the capital investment of a new car, and therefore cannot benefit from improved efficiency gains. In both cases, the individuals who are buying are making intelligent choices within the options available to them. Middle and upper middle-class Americans are buying down, hoping to save on gas and maintenance; the poor are buying their cheap trade-ins. Nevertheless, everyone's intelligence has been and is being muted by a government who sees its role as arbiter of resources rather than informer of the populace. The appropriate role of government in a rapidly changing world should be one of information gathering and dissemination. Part of information is price. If the price of oil is high, that is not a fiction, an abstract, or even a plot. It is the value the world, including America, has placed on a commodity, and market value is information. Rather than shield people from current information, the government should accelerate and improve the flow of information to the citizenry. Given the facts, the American people act with astonishing speed and intelligence.

The important information that is missing today concerns the amount of energy we can have during the next ten years. The debate over whether there is or isn't enough energy in the world obscures the real issue, which is whether we have access to that energy. Dispensing momentarily with the moral dilemma of war, the question is whether it would be wiser to use less or to risk consumption patterns that could lead us into war. It is simplistic to suggest that paying $2 or more per gallon in order to restrict consumption might save the lives of our sons and daughters in combat, but it is appropriate to demonstrate the connectedness between our domestic and individual habits and the foreboding intimations of the headlines.

The nature of the choice process itself points to the outcome. If we choose not to control demand, then the energy decisions will be made by (and for) centralized institutions such as utilities, nuclear power companies, the federal government, utilities commissions, and, of course, oil companies. Increasingly, our fates as individuals will be in the hands of large and distant institutions. An authoritarian outcome is imbedded in the nature of the choice itself.

On the other hand, if we choose to control demand, those choices we make as individuals — where we live, how we live, what we drive, and what we choose to consume — will remain in our hands. Thus the choice for a free society requires the expression of that freedom itself through choices that are responsible to realities of the present.

Keeping all of the foregoing in mind, we would recommend the following:

1. Immediately cut our international imports of oil by much higher energy taxes with rebates.

2. Build no more nuclear plants.

3. Maintain and operate carefully all existing nuclear plants since closing them now will not significantly reduce the risks of nuclear energy.

4. Convert existing oil-fired plants to coal wherever possible and environmentally feasible.

5. Decontrol all energy prices.

6. Provide tax incentives for all forms of energy conservation, e.g., tax credits for weatherizing, insulation, etc.

7. Provide continuing tax credits for all forms of renewable energy, especially solar hot water and space heating.

8. Develop a moderate, well-timed, carefully managed synthetic fuel program.

9. Pursue research and development at a maximum level on all forms of renewable energy and reduce the priority of nuclear fission and nuclear fusion research.

If we fail to adopt at least some if not most of the preceding recommendations, then we commit ourselves to what we have called the Official Future: a high-growth path with a high dependency on imported oil and a high likelihood of military confrontation. If we reduce our energy demands, then what we call a Voluntary History remains available to us. The differences between the Official Future and a Voluntary History in terms of supply and demand of energy are quite dramatic. The differences between their probable social structures are just as dramatic: centralized planning toward a war-minded economy and potential authoritarianism, or a highly diversified economy making the most efficient use of energy.

As commonsensical as these recommendations may be, most of them command little attention in the present policy of the United States government. Prior to the fall of the Shah and the seizure of the hostages, the Carter administration announced the so-called

Carter Doctrine, a statement of U.S. policy calling for us to defend our "vital interest" in the Persian Gulf in order to secure resources. This is one of the few Carter policies that was not only not renounced by the Reagan administration, but made more emphatic. Although we have fought for resources before, we have as a nation always added other issues to the fray, issues such as democracy and liberty. This is the first time that an American president has *stated* that we will fight for a substance rather than a principle, and it is a grave departure from our own principles as articulated in the Constitution and the Declaration of Independence. It is almost an assertion of fighting for dependence rather than its historic opposite. In the case of the Carter Doctrine, we have construed our vital interests as including Saudi light crude. We seem willing to risk war in order to maintain a standard of consumption for the near term that is impossible to maintain over the long term.

The unfortunate implication of such a policy is made more pressing by the dual and conflicting circumstances of rising U.S. demand for foreign oil from countries that cannot afford to raise their supplies. If America were simultaneously making great efforts to reduce its reliance on foreign oil, the claim that a cutoff of imports would unfairly endanger the republic might carry with it some moral weight. But when 5 percent of the world's population consumes nearly a third of its energy, the other 95 percent are not likely to see the morality of the 5 percent's demands for more energy. If we insist on gaining by might what we cannot have by right, then we risk nuclear war. The likelihood of that outcome increases precisely to the extent that we fail to solve our energy problem. To that specter, which has haunted several of our scenarios, we now turn.

Chapter XI

Limited Insanity: On the Prospects of Nuclear War

C LEARLY THERE WOULD BE something disingenuous about a book on the future that failed to confront the possibility of nuclear destruction. Just as clearly, the well-intentioned wish for total disarmament may be no solution but a species of naivete. Granting the insanity of nations poised on the brink of "mutually assured destruction" — MAD was the Defense Department's acronym for our former policy of deterrence by the prospect of all-out destruction — the need for therapy demands that we understand the methods of our madness, the rationality of what seems so insane. Even removing the tools of nuclear war would not undo the causes that led to their development. Nor is their total removal a possibility. The technology remains in the minds of too many.

The proximate cause for the mounting likelihood of war today is the dependency of the industrialized nations on oil from an unstable part of the world. Furthermore, the illusion of control and the dream of victory may prompt oil-importing nations to start conflicts they cannot stop. The transition from the bipolar politics of superpowers to a multipolar world involving many agents makes the prospect of controlling events and outcomes even more elusive.

The likelihood of a limited war turning into nuclear war has increased as a result of changes in U.S. and Soviet defense policies. Perhaps the key indicator of the possibility of this new image of war is Presidential Directive Fifty-nine. Directive Fifty-nine, issued by President Carter in the summer of 1980, is not so much a change in policy as an acknowledgment of a change in policy that had been gradually evolving during the seventies. By itself it was not a decisive action, but rather the recognition that a new policy was indeed in effect. Previously the nuclear policy of the United States had held that if we or our allies or our interests were attacked by nuclear weapons, we would totally destroy the Soviet Union. We had the means to do so: over one thousand Minuteman missiles, most carrying multiple warheads; 656 missiles on submarines, most carrying multiple warheads; and hundreds of long-range bombers carrying high-megaton bombs, some soon to carry Cruise missiles. This vast arsenal of nuclear warheads was designed to destroy the Soviet Union entirely — its population, its agricultural and industrial centers, the nation. The theory held that the Soviet Union would not risk such total annihilation and therefore would not use weapons at all, much less in a limited way.

However, during the seventies, the Soviet Union spent $240 billion more on preparation for war than the United States. They now approach parity in the strength of such strategic forces as missiles and have a clear superiority in conventional weapons. While there is little agreement, most military leaders and many experts argue that this build-up is seen as a sign that the U.S.S.R. no longer sees nuclear holocaust as the only possible outcome of a major conflict with the United States. Otherwise, there would be no point in their vast and expensive preparations for a protracted war. This point of view now guides U.S. policy.

The MAD policy assumed that the Soviet Union would only make an all-out attack on the United States. The dreadful fantasy pictured hundreds of nuclear-tipped missiles coming over the North Pole. Our missiles would then be launched in a massive retaliation: the half-hour holocaust. U.S. policy is now based on the assumption that the Soviets contemplate the use of a much more limited attack, one or two missiles aimed at selected cities or military installations as a tactic in a more conventional war elsewhere, say in Poland. Because our strategic forces are geared to a massive response, the Soviets would believe that we would not retaliate in kind. Massive retaliation would mean the total annihilation of an enemy in response to a limited attack — something that goes against the American grain. More important, it is possible that even an all-out attack would leave sufficient nuclear strike capability in Soviet bombers, submarines, and missiles launched on warning that the United States would probably suffer near if not total annihilation itself. Human life on the planet could be extinguished. As the Soviets consider Americans considering the repugnance of that possibility, the Soviets would believe that their limited first strike might go unanswered. Therefore, Directive Fifty-nine dictates a restructuring and retargeting of American strategic forces to make possible a more limited response striking at Soviet strategic capability with surgical precision. Thus, there emerges a kind of mirror image in which U.S. policy transforms itself to reflect the Soviets'. But no one really knows who is leading and who is following.

What would cause or precipitate such a war? Unfortunately, there are dozens of triggers at the moment. Foremost, as mentioned, is the potential conflict for resources, particularly oil in the Persian Gulf region. Underlying this potential is the fact that from the Russians' point of view, the world looks like a hostile place. We may see the menacing bear spreading across the world landscape, but from Moscow the world looks quite different. Russia sees hostility from China immediately to its southeast, and beyond China is America's strongest Asian ally, Japan. Pakistan, Afghanistan, Iraq, Iran, and Turkey are strongly Islamic and bear little love for white Russia. The East European nations continue to chafe under the Soviet yoke; the Ostpolitik of West Germany is a conscious step in the growing movement for the reunification of Germany; and beyond lie France, Italy, and England; still further west is the vast military, economic, and political might of the United States, whose technology outstrips it, whose economy outperforms it. And wherever Russia looks, in whatever direction, it sees the economic failure of socialism. In the eyes of a hungry world, the ideology of Karl Marx is a fading promise.

Former Secretary of Defense Harold Brown testified before the Congress that a limited nuclear exchange would inevitably escalate to all out nuclear war. In spite of any preparation for limited nuclear war, he felt, it would not stop there and could only end in holocaust. Thus in the end the argument merely becomes a new variation of the old policy of MAD. No one will risk all out war, hence, weapons will not be used. Hence, the danger of war is not increased. But military leaders have often prepared for yesterday's war. The British defenders of Singapore were so certain that because every invasion had always come from the sea, the Japanese would follow precedent. But after a successful march through the jungle of the Malay Peninsula, the Japanese captured Singapore because its defenses pointed seaward.

Today's military preparations for war are fought not in reality but in the mock environments of imagined conflicts. Scenarios found their first use in military planning exercises. "What if the Russians . . . ?" was the question. Today's policy is based on such scenarios. We do not disagree with the conclusion that an escalation to all out nuclear war is the most likely outcome of any nuclear exchange between the U.S. and the Russians. However, we wonder if there may not be a dangerous "jungle side" here. The current policy may lull us into a complacent resumption of the presumed balance of terror. But if we should find ourselves in the reality of armed conflict with the Soviet Union, our behavior may be quite different from yesterday's "imagined wars." The certainty of predictable outcomes is not an assumption we share. One of the lessons of the scenarios is that complex events have unpredictable consequences. There may be other outcomes of limited exchanges. In the following discussion we do not argue the inevitability of limited nuclear war, only that in evaluating the costs and risks of our choices we ought to be aware of the possible consequences.

In entertaining the consequences of a remotely possible "limited" nuclear war, our strategy is to show the absurdity of considering such an exchange as tightly circumscribed — even if it were not to escalate to all-out holocaust. These caveats on our strategy are essential. Without them our consideration of a scenario we regard as a remote and horrendous possibility would play into the hands of those who regard the prospect of a limited nuclear war as a rationale for more weapons. We think planning for limited nuclear war is a mistake. We, therefore, consider the prospect of limited nuclear war not as a probability for which we must plan and arm ourselves, but as a remote possibility which, even in the unlikely case of its remaining "limited," would still amount to a horrible disaster, not a standoff, much less a victory.

Given the precarious state of the world today, it is not difficult to imagine the outbreak of a limited nuclear war. The following list shows a number of current conflicts that could serve as triggers of war:

1. Uprisings in Poland, Korea, Philippines, and El Salvador. (If the U.S. becomes militarily involved in El Salvador, we may see a reverse domino effect: the progressive militarization and polarization of Central America, the Caribbean, and perhaps Mexico.)

2. Border wars between China and Vietnam, Peru and Ecuador, Vietnam and Cambodia, U.S.S.R. and China, Tanzania and Uganda, Argentina and Chile.

3. Black Africa against South Africa, Israel vs. the Arabs.

4. Terrorists and separatists in Canada, Spain, Ireland, Indonesia, Wales, Uruguay, Argentina, and Iran.

5. Occupation of Afghanistan.

6. Violence in Lebanon, Turkey, Cambodia, and Italy.

7. Unstable military regimes in Liberia, Ethiopia, and Korea.

The most likely trigger would be the Middle East. For example, an anti-U.S. coup in Saudi Arabia would destabilize the whole region. In such circumstances, loss of production from the

Saudi fields, whether deliberate or by military "accident," would place the Western nations in grave danger. It is likely that French, German, and Italian troops would be drawn into the Persian Gulf. Any spreading of the conflict toward Iran or Iraq would be the entry point for a Russian presence, if not invasion. Since the bulk of Russian oil is extracted immediately across from the Iranian border, they could feel threatened if they did not take some kind of strong action to counter Western military presence. American forces would almost certainly be drawn in, not only to counter the Russian threat, but to try to re-establish a "normal" flow of oil from Saudi fields now controlled by rightists or leftists.

The withdrawal of troops from Europe would weaken an already weak NATO. If tensions were running high, and they probably would, Russia might invade West Germany through the East German military. It is not clear given such a scenario who would support whom. For some, the growing German strength and the potential reunification of the two Germanies represent as much cause for concern as they do jubilation. A 1980 Army War College study cited an observation on the desirable size of the German military: "They should be strong enough to scare the Russians but not so strong that they would frighten the French." (That same study noted Francois Mauriac's comment, "I love Germany so much, I am overjoyed there are two.") Would the Eastern bloc nations remain in the Warsaw Pact? Would Russia be strong enough militarily to prevent Polish and Czechoslovakian resistance? Would Holland rush to Germany's aid or remain ambivalent?

In a spreading grid of conflict, China may be emboldened to recapture territories it has contested with Russia. It is not clear where the nuclear frontier might be breached. Russia might be tempted to deploy nuclear weapons first in a precisely aimed strike at China's fledgling nuclear capability. Since Russian troop movements would be large and bulky, they would pose tempting targets for nuclear strikes. Western forces may decide that they have no choice except to strike back with tactical nuclear weapons intended to stop any further troop movement. In such moments of profound tension, technological or human errors could also trigger a wider war. Instead of directly attacking the United States, Russia might launch nuclear-tipped missiles at the Polaris submarine base in Scotland. With the nuclear frontier breached, the structure of warfare would shift from direct, large-scale, land confrontations to limited thrusts of small quantities of troops, ships, aircraft, and missiles against a background of enormous tension, fear, and calculation. A war could develop in which limited advantage would be sought by limited means, but nuclear weapons would be among those means. The earlier logic that mutually assured destruction would prevent confrontation changes into a thrust and parry war that extends indefinitely into a bleak future.

No one wants to use nuclear weapons, but the uncontrollability of the situation means that tactical nuclear weapons would be introduced into the inevitable logic of the war. As each party acts in its interest, the consequences become insane for the whole.

We do not wish to develop this horrible fantasy into a full scenario; a sketch suffices to make our point. Although such a war is not inevitable, it is possible. And once started it could persist for a long time. The unraveling of alliances, the restructuring of complex relationships and sets of interests having to do in part with oil, the security of the Soviet borders, ideological differences, cultural and racial differences — all could combine in a continuing series of such conflicts in a ring around the Soviet Union and in other parts of Africa, Latin America, South America, and Asia. A highly complex and protracted war in which there would be limited nuclear exchanges in order to achieve particular strategic objectives is distressingly plausible.

Such a war would have profound domestic implications. The United States would have to sustain a high-level war economy. Every once in a while some part of the country, or perhaps an allied country, would be hit with nuclear weaponry. Not only would we be facing war; we would be carrying a shelter mentality, a perpetual sense of doom and insecurity. No one would know when one's particular part of the country might be a victim of a limited nuclear holocaust. We would come to loathe the Soviet Union with a passion that could lead us into distorted political forms. We would be trapped by our own technology, as we would have to endure a protracted period of nuclear contamination and destruction for fear that any change in the rules or stakes would mean instant annihilation. The erosion of freedom, the very subversion of a national *raison d'etre,* would destroy America as much as would the poisons of the war.

The tale is not far removed from Orwell's *Nineteen Eighty-four.* Gray is the color of this future. We could face war for decades, perhaps a century. It has taken decades to create a world so capable of war and so hostile to itself. Although we cannot quickly avert the consequences of the choices made over preceding decades, there are actions that we can take today that can avert long-range consequences. It is precisely our feelings of impotence in the face of current forces leading toward war that can provide the motive for gaining power over our more distant future.

Recognizing the realities of a world in which hostility persists beyond all desires for peace, we cannot ignore the need for some weapons. But we can pursue less self-destructive policies in our choice of weapons. A massive strategic arsenal and an immense standing army were the necessary tools of a policy based on "mutually assured destruction" and "containment." The experiences of Vietnam, Iran, and Afghanistan, combined with the growing strength of France, Germany, Britain, and even some Third World nations, should be sufficient to cast doubt upon policies based on the prospect of simply overpowering our adversaries with sheer military might. A dozen different investigations all question the level of effectiveness of the conventional forces. In 1980, out of a fleet of thirteen aircraft carriers at sea, nine were rated by DOD as only "marginally" capable, while the remaining four were "not ready" for combat. The navy has 15,000 spots for petty officers unfilled in ships at sea. Six of ten army divisions were also rated as unready, and only half the air force's fighters are "mission capable."

A defense policy to go with a new concept of national security must deal with strategic and conventional forces as well as with the issue of the draft. The Strategic Arms Limitations Treaty (SALT) negotiations with the U.S.S.R. should be pushed in the direction of actual reductions of nuclear arsenals. No one yet expects the elimination of nuclear weapons, but reducing the likelihood of total destruction seems possible. By the early nineties, agreements could be reached that would eliminate all long-range bombers by the year 2000. All land-based long-range missiles could be eliminated, and both sides could reduce the number of submarine-based missiles by 30 percent or more. (It is not implausible to limit the development of new technology for strategic weapons.) The policy would amount to allowing the aging of technology to determine the schedule for phasing it out. Old devices would retire from service without replacement by new, more sophisticated weapons.

Our conventional forces need a thorough revamping. A general strategy might limit the size and improve the quality. The total standing forces could be slowly reduced by 50 percent in numbers of units and personnel while the level of training, salary, support, and equipment for the remaining forces were significantly upgraded. By the early nineties the size of the military could be one million men and women compared to over two million a decade before. Civilian staff could be reduced. Costs would not go down much, however. Quality improvements are not cheap. High technology would be used where appropriate (for instance, intelligence task forces), but basic weaponry — tanks, transports — should be kept simple, repairable, often small and cheap, hence replaceable. The XM-1 tank, the C-5 transport, and the F-15 are weapons that are so expensive as to be irreplaceable — hence not usable — and so sophisticated as to be unreliable. The esprit and morale of the military would probably rise rapidly as they regained confidence in their own competence and reliability. Americans could feel a sense of commitment to genuine strength, and military service could become a legitimate professional career once more.

If we acknowledge the need for a military of a sizable scale, then we must face another issue. A military composed only of volunteers who are paid enough seems inappropriate in a democratic society and carries with it the potential danger of an autonomous mercenary force. Yet the authors are all from a generation that fought conscription in the era of the Vietnam War. A strong ethical argument can be made against any form of conscription. Furthermore, one cannot separate the issue entirely from foreign policy. A policy that is legitimate will be able to draw enough support that even a draft will be attainable. Vietnam lacked that legitimacy. World War II did not. Even so most of our allies (and potential adversaries) have some form of conscription, even universal service. We may not be able to avoid it. Yet the alternatives of inadequate defense or a purely professional military are equally inadequate. We could avoid the hard issues of national security vs. conscientious resistance to the draft by trying to convince ourselves that one of the three alternatives is not so bad after all: either we don't need much of a fighting force, because the world is perfectly safe for democracy; or a professional military would not be dangerous; or the draft isn't all that offensive. But we, the authors, cannot bring ourselves to believe any of these rationalizations for softening the conflict. Consequently, we propose that we find some way of expanding the pool of trained personnel without requiring that everyone be trained to kill.

The country needs people trained in teamwork and logistics, not only for warfare but for civil defense and disaster relief. An expanded and redirected National Guard could satisfy the demand for a large pool of minimally trained personnel that could be mobilized in wartime. In peacetime, such a force could engage in labor-intensive domestic projects: rebuilding roads, refurbishing housing, reclaiming desert, all the while standing ready for well-rehearsed hurricane and earthquake emergency relief. Training in basic survival skills could supplement the academic and technical education of the public school system. National needs in the areas of energy and food might be addressed both educationally and through hands-on action. Finally, such a service would play an important and updated role as a socializing institution. In our increasingly diverse society, bonds based on shared work might be increasingly important.

No matter how we revamp our military, however, no improvements of personnel or technology will make us secure, or save as many lives as staying out of war altogether. The prospect of peace offers more genuine security than the prospect of winning a war. Granted that an important part of avoiding war is maintaining a preparedness that renders others reluctant to rattle swords, we contend that for deterrence purposes *we are strong enough*. We can destroy any part of the world at will. Therefore the question of national security should not be restricted to calculations of megatonnage.

No longer at the pinnacle of power, the United States is now one very powerful nation among others. Its security is inextricably linked to the successful development and well-being of its trading partners and allies around the world. The most fundamental point is the recognition that even in a world that is not yet ready to forego violence as an instrument of policy, mutual terror is no basis for mutual security. Genuine strength, mutual respect, and shared development provide a firmer ground for both peace and the protection of individual interests. Our strength should rely more on our political and economic stance toward other nations and less on military power. We cannot detail a total U.S. foreign and military policy. We can suggest in a sketchy fashion some of the basic principles and provide examples of a policy that would recognize current and future economic and political realities, reduce the likelihood of war, and preserve basic American values.

Two examples will serve to suggest the nature of a more realistic and appropriate foreign policy. The United States could establish a program of political and economic agreements with Mexico on the scale of a Marshall Plan. To be sure, overcoming a century of antipathy between the two cultures will not be easy. Nor will identifying appropriate developmental goals be a simple matter. But major development efforts by the United States in Mexico cannot only help Mexico; it can fuel growth here as trade increases. Increased trade might have the added advantages of relieving tensions along our shared border.

Carlos Fuentes, the Mexican diplomat, offered another example when, in an interview with Bill Moyers, he pointed out a critical flaw in the U.S. response to the Soviet invasion of Afghanistan. The real threat he said was more vital to the Third World than to the United States or other industrial nations, but the United States took the mantle of leadership for itself, even knowing it could do nothing, in effect becoming spokesperson for a constituency that was absent. Fuentes suggested that if we had helped some of the stronger Third World countries, such as Mexico, Indonesia, or Pakistan, take the lead, these countries could have become more effective partners of the United States in maintaining the balance of power.

National security and issues of defense policy are usually regarded as synonymous. But our world-spanning military could not free the American hostages in Tehran or raise the value of the dollar. A broadened definition of the arena of national security is needed. The United States can no longer safely assume that its intrinsic economic superiority and political stature can assure it access to markets and resources, or that, all else failing, its military can guarantee that access. Our national security now depends on the competitiveness of our businesses against our allies, the Germans and the Japanese; the attitude of our energy-rich neighbors to the north and south; what the OPEC oil ministers believe about our willingness and resolve to conserve energy and develop alternatives to imported oil; what the conflict-torn people of South Africa believe about who should get access to their immense treasure of minerals; and other factors. National security now must deal with economics, culture, and politics in a long-term strategic sense.

Our reduced relative economic and political stature now requires that we:

1. Identify our own future with the future of other people all

over the world, developing long-term stable economic, cultural, and political relationships that are not subject to the fate of a particular regime either here or abroad.

2. Develop and implement a coherent, consistent international trade and finance strategy.

3. Deal with our allies from a position of equality rather than superiority — we must be more consistent and less arrogant, and they must shoulder more responsibility for world peace.

4. Recognize that the U.S.S.R. will exploit political instability around the world, but that it is rarely, if ever, the sole cause of that instability.

5. Be prepared for and be willing to respond to the real threats that may require military action.

These recommendations, in addition to the earlier suggestions for refurbishing the military, reducing our energy dependence, and restoring our relationships with the Third World, all presuppose a healthy economy. In the next chapter we address the issue of the ailing American economy.

Chapter XII

Cultural Economics

PPROPRIATELY ENOUGH, the Reagan presidency began with talk of an "economic Dunkirk." The insecurity in the energy system that leads to freshening of the winds of war is mirrored in economic insecurity. A decade of mounting inflation, interest rates, and unemployment, and declining income, productivity, and economic influence have all led to a growing sense of uncertainty about the future. The uncertainty is well founded. There are, indeed, some very basic economic changes under way, both in economic realities and in our approach to analyzing and managing the economy.

In recent years a number of analysts have succeeded in demonstrating that the fundamental tenets of Keynesian and neo-Keynesian economics are inadequate. The dynamics of supply and demand may explain the microeconomic behavior of price fluctuations in particular markets. But the macroeconomics of nations over decades defy the simple nostrums of Keynesian demand management. Government spending succeeded in "priming the pump" to get money flowing during the thirties, and higher interest rates seemed to inhibit demand, thereby retarding inflation, during periods of rapid expansion in the sixties and seventies. But, as a report of the Joint Economic Committee conceded in 1980, "fine tuning" the economy by federally imposed demand management failed to cope with the anomaly of stagflation: high unemployment (inducing low demand) combined with high inflation (presumably as a result of high demand). Neither monetarist policies influencing the money supply, nor make-work programs aimed at unemployment have halted the reductions in real wages and profits.

The basic engine of the economy has been the production of increasing amounts of material goods at a lower price for more people. The cornucopia of material goods available to the American consumer spilled forth from complex interactions among cheap resources, rapidly expanding markets, ready access to capital, technological innovation, and hard work. Now that resources are rising rapidly in price, birthrates are declining, and consumer markets are nearing saturation, we can expect, and we are seeing, a reversal of market patterns: people are only able to buy a few goods at higher prices, and they don't like it. Does this mean that high rates of growth may be nearing an end and does that portend changes in production and consumption patterns?

As long as productivity increased, consumers could borrow against rising incomes to finance current consumption wants. But it takes productivity growth to repay those loans, and with declining productivity we are becoming saddled with both burdensome debt and the inability to raise sufficient capital to invest in newer technology to improve our productivity. Inflation may have made our debts easier to face, but it has made capital ever more elusive, hence investment in productivity ever more unlikely, hence a defensive shift from production to consumption ever more inevitable. We are not likely to invest in productivity because we are spending too much for government services, from transfer payments to current defense expenditures, on top of paying off the debt for the war in Vietnam. Corporations are too eager to report profits rather than re-invest in productivity, and individuals, too, prefer consuming to saving. We have played a game of mirrors on ourselves until we have confused image with reality, inflation with wealth. For homeowners, inflation and low interest rates increase the values of their homes enough to allow them to finance more consumption — so why stop inflation? For government, inflation makes it unnecessary to set priorities. Everybody can have everything because tax revenues increase with rising wages. But finally many workers are realizing that while their incomes have more than doubled, their purchasing power has risen by only 10 percent. We hid the cost of energy by regulating its price so that we failed to make necessary efficiency improvements. We became less productive in the process. Hiding the costs of environmental quality has further added to the inflationary spiral of declining productivity and inefficient investment. Environmental quality is not a luxury, however much business might wish it were so. We have erected a costly environmental regulatory apparatus rather than tackling the necessary costs head on.

Lately, a number of economists, government officials and business leaders have called attention to the problem of declining productivity. The new school of so-called supply-side economics would have no quarrel with the preceding critique of neo-Keynesian demand-management. Likewise, supply-side economists would agree that declining productivity is among the most fundamental causes of inflation. The very term, "supply-side," connotes a strategy of closing the gap between high demand and low supply not by reducing demand — the neo-Keynesian formula — but by increasing supply through increasing productivity. But the primary tools of supply-side economic policy management are the tools inherited from Keynesian theory: federal manipulation of interest rates and tax structures in accordance with diagnoses derived from the traditional economic indicators. Tax cuts are expected to stimulate economic activity enough to increase profits; the government will get a slightly smaller share of larger incomes — enough to balance the budget, reduce federal borrowing, ease the demand for credit, stimulate private sector investment, raise productivity, reduce inflation, and so on around the circle of traditional economic rationality.

Rather than re-enter that same circle from the side of supply rather than demand, however, we suggest expanding the circle of economic categories to include more of the factors that affect the economy. We are not arguing that either neo-Keynesian or supply-side economists are necessarily wrong in their analyses of the economic interactions they examine. The point is rather that some significant factors have been left out of the economic picture. Economists tend to see only as much as their tools can measure and manipulate. If their categories fail to include some significant variables, then no amount of tinkering with the old levers will be adequate to new realities.

The bankruptcy of classical economics has stimulated a number of analysts to look beyond the usual variables in order to explain the behavior of the economy. Nicholas Georgescu-Roegen, Barry Commoner, and others have emphasized the oddities of the role of energy. Since traditional supply and demand theory uses *current* supply and demand to determine current prices, it fails to take account of the difference between renewable and nonrenewable supplies. Hence its failure to predict rising prices of nonrenewable resources. Furthermore, the economic abstraction called the Gross National Product fails to measure the energy efficiency of production: not the dollar cost but the energy cost of production.

In a nutshell, newer theories are needed to relate economy to ecology. Features that were earlier dismissed as "externalities," like environmental pollution, are now coming home to roost. An expanded theory is required that will relate not only the supply and demand for capital, labor, goods, and services, but also for natural resources.

As biologist Garrett Hardin has argued, the management of scarce resources is everyone's business and therefore no one's business. As Hardin's persuasive analysis of "the tragedy of the commons" indicates, the rational pursuit of individual interests (equals profits) will inevitably lead to the depletion of common resources to the detriment of all. Therefore, argue Commoner, Ivan Illich, and others, social planning for social needs must replace the pursuit of profits if we are to increase the efficient use of resources, change the ratio of energy use to production, and thereby revive our economy.

Our analysis suggests otherwise. We, too, acknowledge the need for an economic theory that includes among its variables more than figures on the short-term supply and demand of capital and labor, goods and services. We, too, acknowledge the need for the more efficient use of scarce resources to satisfy those social needs dismissed as "externalities." But if efficiency in the use of scarce resources is the answer, we question whether socialism, as classically conceived, has any better prospect than capitalism as a solution to the dilemma of stagflation. Socialism, the solution explicitly advocated by Commoner, Illich and many others, does not have a good track record for efficiency.

Granting the point that the capitalist pursuit of consumption and short-term profits leads to a long-run decline of productivity, it does not follow that a planned economy will utilize resources any more efficiently than a free enterprise economy. If anything, recent history suggests quite the opposite. Japan and West Germany have outperformed Russia and East Germany, and England's move toward socialism has been an economic disaster. The lesson of recent history seems to suggest that a new economic theory needs to expand not only by incorporating the externalities of energy and ecology, but that a new theory must also find ways to include the almost intangible — therefore previously ignored — factors of cultural values.

The economic miracles of post-war Japan and Germany depend at least in part on deeply imbued traditions of hard work and cultural solidarity. It cannot be a coincidence that the countries currently making the greatest gains in productivity are countries where relatively homogeneous values reinforce a willingness to work in cooperation *and* competition. While the U.S.S.R. and the United States have acted out the extremes of collectivism and individualism respectively, each clinging to its own ideological extreme of forced cooperation or laissez-faire competition, Japan and Germany have evolved toward political economies in which the glib distinction between private and public sectors has been overcome — but not in the direction of socialism. Instead, an atmosphere of intense competition has been maintained, but without the social inefficiencies associated with either bureaucratic Soviet socialism or laissez-faire profit-mongering.

Where the United States has relied on adversary relationships to stimulate competition in a free enterprise economy, "Japan, Inc." and the practice of codetermination in German labor relations provide models of cooperation within what remain free-market economies. Without excessive down-from-the-top bureaucratic administration, Germany and Japan have managed to achieve forms of cooperation between labor and management on the one hand, government and business on the other. Despite their remarkable successes in their own national traditional contexts, however, the Japanese and German models may be inappropriate to the less homogeneous American setting.

If we are to extend the domain of political-economic theory beyond the variables of supply and demand to include both resource allocation and cultural values, then we must confront the overwhelmingly obvious fact that the United States is a country consisting of highly heterogeneous groups. We cannot appeal to any unified set of values to galvanize such a diverse population into higher productivity. Instead, we seem beset with a "zero-sum" society in which, as economist Lester Thurow argues, one group can improve its lot only at the expense of some other group. Since we seem to lack the will to make the hard decisions of loss allocation, our diversity takes the form of mutually imposed paralysis: no group will let any other group get away with anything. This crisis of mutually imposed impotence applies to the adversary relationships between labor and management, business and government, consumer groups and producers, doctors and patients. Our adversary culture has increased the cost of almost everything from health to insurance to automobiles.

To summarize the current paradox within a dilemma: on one horn we have the problem of productivity, on the other our adversary culture. Within the problem of productivity, we acknowledge the need for planning to counteract the unrestrained pursuit of individual gain at the cost of the collective, yet we contend that the resort to socialism will generate inefficiencies leading to low productivity. So we conclude that we need something like the Japanese or German reliance on culturally cohesive ideals to stimulate productivity without resorting to socialist bureaucracy. Yet when we turn from the horn of bloodless economics, where the paradox of stagflation forces us to expand our economic categories toward ecology and beyond, we then confront the other horn of the dilemma: the beyond of culturally cohesive values which seems unavailable to Americans, for whom diversity is more highly valued than unity or homogeneity. How can we supplement market mechanisms with some degree of anticipatory planning when we are both unwilling to fall back on a managed economy and unable to appeal to a common tradition of cohesive values?

The horns of this dilemma are sharpest when we insist on coming down on one side or the other. The debate between planners and proponents of free enterprise has the form of a dilemma only when posed as a disjunctive either/or. In fact, we already live in what has come to be known as a "mixed" economy. And "convergence" is the term used to characterize the way the Soviets are learning the virtues of the profit motive at the same time capitalist economies are learning to plan.

The idea of accommodation need not require concession or surrender of one's own values. It is a question of understanding precisely how one's own values require their opposite — how one's own preferences would be better fulfilled if others prefer the contrary. The point is obvious in such instances as the choice of hiking trails: one can enjoy a degree of solitude *only* if others prefer to be somewhere else. The point is nonetheless true in less obvious cases like the contrariety between masculine and feminine. We do not need to decide which is "right." Neither is right unless both are.

The trouble with an adversarial approach to certain issues is that accommodation smacks of compromise. Even where the issue at hand is one where a synthesis of extremes would be richer than either extreme by itself, merely setting up the issue as a sharp dichotomy prejudges the mode of its resolution: either/or, not both/and. To be more specific, though we live in what is in fact a mixed economy, our attachment to adversarial extremes often blinds us to the advantages of a real synthesis. So the proponents of each extreme vainly attempt to retain pockets of ideological turf where their values are uncompromised. The result is, in the language of chemistry, a mixture, not a solution. In our "mixed" economy, the contrary elements do not truly join in a solution to the problem of stagflation. Precisely where we need a market economy to stimulate innovation and efficiency, for example, in the administration of social services, we see massive and inefficient bureaucracies. Precisely where we need greater planning, in the area of energy, we see conflict between the government and the competing interests of the oil companies locked in a stalemate that serves only OPEC.

There will be no solution to these problems as long as they are fought on the field of a knock-down, drag-out battle between socialism and capitalism. Victory for either side — partial or total — is really defeat because plans and profits must be complementary, not disjunctive. This much the Japanese and Germans have demonstrated. But how, with our more heterogeneous culture, can we learn the same lessons?

We believe that the most hopeful course in the decades ahead depends upon our willingness and ability to decentralize some of the basic institutions of American society. While a great deal has been written about the advantages of economies of scale, according to which big is purportedly beautiful, profitable, and efficient, recent years have witnessed a whole series of phenomena demonstrating upper limits to institutional growth. These limits are not only ecological but organizational, social, and psychological. There comes a point of diminishing returns beyond which the economic and political advantages that accrue to larger organizations are offset by organizational inefficiencies resulting from sheer size. These organizational inefficiencies are not well understood, partly because they have to do with factors that are not easy to quantify, for example, psychological issues of loyalty, devotion, and self-esteem. Nevertheless, it is becoming increasingly clear that some of our political, educational, medical, and economic institutions have reached a scale at which the ostensible advantages of size no longer produce the desired results. Instead, diseconomies of scale follow from lack of flexibility, failures of communication and relevant information access, increasing costs of distribution, and human alienation from institutions that dwarf human scale.

In addition to its cost effectiveness and efficiency, appropriate decentralization offers a solution to the problem of internalizing cultural ideals into an expanded theory of economics. If the strength and cohesiveness of the German and Japanese cultures figure in their post-war economic recovery, does that mean that the United States, with its manifest heterogeneity, is condemned to a choice between a sluggish zero-sum economy or recovery at the cost of unprecedented authoritarian planning? Not if decentralization is as cost effective as we think it can be in the United States. For decentralization is the organizational structure most appropriate to our ideological tradition of freedom.

Freedom itself is not a cultural value in the same sense as the specific traditions of German or Japanese culture. Freedom, in a federalist system, is instead the opportunity to pursue any of several possible traditions. Freedom cannot be construed as license to do anything at all, within or without a tradition. That way lies anarchy. Freedom, in a decentralized setting, is the opportunity to define local norms for behavior. It is an opportunity for communities to carry on different traditions.

Decentralization of authority does not have to devolve from the centralized state all the way down to the individual. Intermediate groups of various sizes are, in America, the repositories of the values and traditions that give freedom its social meaning. By decentralizing some of our economic institutions down to a structural level commensurate with our cultural pluralism, we can draw upon the strengths of different traditions.

A whole bibliography from Percival and Paul Goodman's *Communitas* (1947) to Leopold Kohr's *The Breakdown of Nations* (1957), E. F. Schumacher's *Small Is Beautiful* (1973), James Ogilvy's *Many Dimensional Man: Decentralizing Self, Society, and the Sacred* (1977), and Kirkpatrick Sale's *Human Scale* (1980) has argued the advantages of limiting the size of our basic institutions. Indeed the rising popularity of polemics for decentralization raises the problem that we may dismantle some of our institutions with the same one-sided zeal that generated their gargantuan growth.

Neither big nor small is always and inevitably beautiful. As with technology, romantic enthusiasms for and against are less helpful than careful assessments of appropriateness in particular cases. Cottage industry is inappropriate to the production of ships. Conversely, as suggested in our scenario Living Within Our Means, products like soap and toothpaste are easy to manufacture and package in local facilities that obviate the need for advertising and expensive transportation and distribution.

In the years ahead, American culture may give way to increasing diversification among different areas and different sectors of our society, some centralized and some decentralized. Detailed content analyses of hundreds of local newspapers indicate that the tide has already turned toward decentralization. Social movements like the rising interest in ecology owe more to a kind of whispering campaign in the hustings than to any loudspeakers in Washington, New York, or Los Angeles. The media giants, particularly the TV networks, now face a technological revolution in electronic communications whose outcome will be a proliferation of local programming and special interest channels: narrowcasting in place of broadcasting. These developments in technology and the media arrive in the wake of the myth of America as a melting pot. Ethnic identity, racial pride, gender consciousness and generational awareness are carving our society into an ever finer grid of groupings.

Clearly there is a danger that increasing heterogeneity and decentralization in American society may turn us into a nation of mutually destructive factions. There are those who claim that interest-group politics incapacitate our legislative process. But a brighter possibility may lie barely hidden beneath the appearance of social disintegration.

Following an awkward post-war period, a successful America outgrew the bonds of personal loyalty and devotion. The country became so large, its character so diffuse, that the youth of the fifties and sixties could no longer encompass its scale in feelings of attachment and patriotism. A human capacity for devotion went begging amidst talk of countercultural alienation from the behemoth. Now the capacity for devotion, recently curled back upon itself in narcissistic self-involvement, can once again find groups of a manageable size and discernible identity, from ethnic groups to neighborhoods, special interest groups, clubs, local athletic teams, corporations, food co-ops, and intentional communities. The nation has fragmented and multiplied into a whole range of repositories for group loyalty. And so much the better that these new groupings are not nations with separate armies.

Conflicts abound, and they will persist. But we need not deplore the fact that many people feel attachments that inspire passion and dedication. The point of this section has been to suggest that, because we can no longer hide from the reality of hard choices, bloodless economics needs to be infused with an appreciation for the role such passions play in the great drama of productivity and growth. The next chapter will reflect upon the attitudes required if we are to keep these potentially benign passions from devolving into destructive conflicts. The intent of both chapters is to suggest the lineaments of a pluralistic society with a decentralized economy, one that might make fewer demands on the international politics of energy. The goal of avoiding war unfolds into the logic of regional groups tapping unique enthusiasms to inspire and sustain interlocking economies.

Chapter XIII
Conclusion

NATIONS AND PEOPLES MOVE AHEAD and prosper when a common vision inspires their progress. The remarkable post-war recoveries made by Japan and Germany bear witness to the economic potential of sheer people power. Human resources are finally the most irreplaceable of all; the ideas, inventions, and beliefs that motivate a people add more to their well-being than the sheer brawn of labor power. The record of human progress shows how intelligence and ingenuity can accomplish more than muscle and sweat. But intelligence and ingenuity also require motivation, for instance, the challenge of national recovery after a devastating loss, or the shared goals of a culture with common ideals. In short, some sense of vision or purpose can inspire a people to economic wonders, however handicapped they may be by shortages of capital and/or natural resources.

The ambitious plan of this final chapter is to define a vision for America. This ambition would be pretentious if we claimed to compose that vision from whole cloth. Quite to the contrary, the task at hand is a matter of reminding Americans of the visions and values already deeply entrenched in our culture; not to invent anew, but to recall and refine some of our oldest beliefs, and to reinterpret their appropriateness to a new world. Our strategy is neither to hark back to old nostrums, nor to invent values. Instead our effort acknowledges those characteristics that define the people we have become; takes seriously the new environment of the world as it is now; and articulates a vision of what we might yet become.

The tactics for our strategy involve accommodations on three different fronts. The first two are the traditional Left and Right: the so-called liberal and conservative wings of an outdated spectrum that no longer defines the whole range of options in today's world. A third force has recently performed the service of moving public debate away from obsolete argument between Right and Left. That third force we will call the Transformative Alternative. In its most comprehensive statement, *The Aquarian Conspiracy,* by Marilyn Ferguson, compiles ideas ranging from the physics of Ilya Prigogine to Theodore Roszak's several books, Hazel Henderson's economics, and many other contributions. The Transformative Alternative defines one side of a three-sided controversy to which we add a Voluntary History as a fourth position. Our differences with other positions are not to be reduced to a formulaic opposition on all points. To the contrary, our hope is to render their respective insights more realistic and consequently more powerful. As with our appropriations of many elements from traditional Right and Left, so our assimilation of contributions from the Transformative Alternative aims toward showing how ideological stances can be enriched rather than refuted by reality.

To carry out the strategy of salvaging from the old what remains appropriate to new realities, we have abstracted a set of fundamental values that defines the three positions we hope to synthesize. (See Tables 17, 18, and 19.) Each of these values has some merit in itself, and even more merit when enhanced by the nourishing context of other values with which it is consistent. We maintain that each of the three familiar stances is inevitably inconsistent in the way it attempts to apply its values to the contemporary world. Our vision remains modest in the sense that it requires nothing dramatically new; only a recombination of familiar elements in a pattern that is more consistent with new realities than the other three alternatives.

The values in question include freedom, social order, diversity, power, predictability, and peace. Each of these values represents some clearly discernible good. Unfortunately, not all good things

Table 17
The Right Wing

Preference among basic values: freedom, diversity, order, predictability. *Contradictions:* the range of diversity is highly limited (e.g., moral majority), freedom and order are in conflict in a diverse society.

Attitude toward the future: economic progress through free enterprise; more, bigger, better. *Contradictions:* resource constraints, stagflation, change in values (e.g., quality of life).

Belief about locus of power: individual and corporation. *Contradictions:* conflict of individual autonomy vs. centralized corporate bureaucracy (e.g., sagebrush rebellion vs. oil companies).

Interpretation of key social relationships: the "free" individual and the family. *Contradiction:* individual must subordinate to appropriate authority (e.g., military, "boss," etc.).

Attitude toward the family: the root of society. *Contradiction:* it is often sacrificed to achieve and exploit affluence.

Attitude toward crime: an eye for an eye, justice equals vengeance following a fair trial. *Contradiction:* crime is still rising despite punitive systems.

Attitude toward welfare: charity, but the poor will always be with us. *Contradiction:* the poor are angry and are no longer accepting of their lot — there could again be rioting in the streets.

Attitude toward energy: all-out supply — oil, coal, nuclear, synthetics; "conservation means being too cold in winter and too hot in summer" (Reagan). *Contradiction:* politically, economically, and physically unrealistic and dangerous.

Attitude toward the environment: nature is for man to use (dominion). *Contradiction:* technology cannot overwhelm complex, more enduring ecosystems — we will lose, nature will win.

Attitude toward regulation: an unnecessary constraint on free enterprise. *Contradiction:* business has at times severely abused its freedom (e.g., pollution, worker exploitation, product reliability, and safety) and refused to police itself.

Ideal economy: free enterprise, big business, neo-Keynesian theory, growing service economy. *Contradiction:* the economy is performing consistently very poorly — it isn't working.

Attitude toward national security: we're No. 1, the Russians want to bury us — we're not strong enough — more and bigger of everything. *Contradictions:* we live in a multipolar world — Russians may be real threat — no one is No. 1 — the war of the flea.

Featured lifestyle: upper and middle class. *Contradiction:* not sustainable without a loss of freedom.

Attitude toward health care: high technology for those who can afford it. *Contradictions:* too expensive, increased iatrogenic disease.

Table 18
The Left Wing

Preference among basic values: social welfare, homogeneity/equality, centralized bureaucracy. *Contradiction:* the worldwide failure of socialism (economic stagnation and the Gulag).

Attitude toward the future: planned economic development. *Contradiction:* it isn't working.

Belief about locus of power: centralized bureaucracy and party. *Contradiction:* it is stultifying and moribund.

Interpretation of key social relationships: the collective. *Contradictions:* elites are dominant even in left wing regimes, social democracies, and the "new class" here in U.S.

Attitude toward the family: minimally necessary. *Contradictions:* inadequate social fabric — symptoms such as alcoholism and suicide.

Attitude toward crime: repress dissent in the name of equality, rehabilitation. *Contradiction:* tends toward a police state.

Attitude toward welfare: socialism, economic equality. *Contradiction:* shrinking pieces of a declining pie.

Attitude toward energy: nuclear and oil for hard left — no nukes for the eco-left. *Contradiction:* politically, economically, and physically unrealistic and dangerous.

Attitude toward the environment: exploit for the public good. *Contradictions:* technology cannot overwhelm complex, more enduring ecosystems — we will lose, nature will win.

Attitude toward regulation: a useful social tool — the private good may conflict with public good. *Contradiction:* a highly inefficient economy tends to result.

Ideal economy: the planned industrial economy. *Contradiction:* outperformed by capitalist economies.

Attitude toward national security: wars of liberation, identify with Third World — U.S. is an imperialist power and should disarm. *Contradiction:* Soviet military power and adventurism (e.g., Afghanistan).

Featured lifestyle: the worker, the intellectual, and the liberal upper-middle class. *Contradiction:* the poor aspire to affluence and the affluent feel guilty aspiring to poverty.

Attitude toward health care: national health care. *Contradiction:* further burden on bureaucracy.

Table 19
The Transformational Alternative

Preference among basic values: freedom, diversity within broad limits, spontaneity, peace, human development. *Contradictions:* encourages narcissism and denies reality of conflict, depends on affluence as context.

Attitude toward the future: a planetary transformation, a sea change in values and belief systems. *Contradictions:* degree of social change is proportional to magnitude of forces creating it — transformation requires a major shock — the outcome is more likely worse than better.

Belief about locus of power: decentralized, small-scale, cooperative organizations — a universal spiritual power. *Contradictions:* not everything can be decentralized and not everyone accepts the power of God.

Interpretation of key social relationships: individual liberation and collective participation. *Contradiction:* may devolve to narcissism and denial of conflict.

Attitude toward the family: experimental forms, e.g., extended families. *Contradiction:* the failure of childrearing in alternative schools.

Attitude toward crime: generally ignores crime as a problem.

Attitude toward welfare: ignores poverty except in a generalized notion of sharing.

Attitude toward energy: conservation and renewable energy. *Contradiction:* could not make a radical transformation in energy use patterns fast enough to abandon traditional fossil fuels and current nuclear capacity.

Attitude toward the environment: a romantic pastoral view of man in nature. *Contradiction:* a population of four billion cannot all return to nature.

Attitude toward regulation: generally a good thing, but tend toward decentralized solutions. *Contradiction:* ignores the costs — both social and economic — of regulatory superstructures.

Ideal economy: small businesses, cottage industry, and right livelihood — the dignity of work. *Contradictions:* there are necessarily large-scale businesses and some kinds of work cannot give the worker a sense of value or worth.

Attitude toward national security: there are no real threats, advocate disarmament. *Contradictions:* there are real dangers in the world.

Featured lifestyle: voluntary simplicity and high tech/high touch. *Contradiction:* many more people still prefer life bought in Macy's and Sears, Roebuck.

Attitude toward health care: holistic health. *Contradictions:* there are some useful drugs and surgical practices, herbs will not reset a broken hip, surgically implanted pins can.

go together. A society that stresses diversity may have to sacrifice a degree of social order. Real freedom precludes predictability. Power does not always serve the cause of peace. So the problem facing any culture is the problem of tradeoffs. Collectivist cultures trade individual liberty for social cohesion and predictability. Liberal democracies sacrifice a degree of social planning in order to protect diversity and individual freedom. Furthermore, different sectors of society stand to benefit or lose from the balance of values characterizing a given society as a whole. During the cultural revolution in China, for example, many intellectuals committed suicide rather than sacrifice their liberty to the goal of social egalitarianism.

Though it is unlikely that Americans will make a social choice as dramatic in its consequences as the cultural revolution in China, a broad-based transformation of attitudes along the lines of the Apocalyptic Transformation scenario is within the realm of possibility. The McCarthy era demonstrated our capacity for falling prey to a witch hunt mentality. And less dramatic trends among attitudes toward values may have consequences that are long lasting and therefore ultimately more significant than McCarthyism. We face our own version of a choice between the interests of the mandarins and the interests of the people.

In *An Inquiry into the Human Prospect,* Robert Heilbroner argues that Western civilization cannot persevere. We are inclined to disagree with Heilbroner's bleak forecast. The cast of his current pessimism is ironically similar to the error of his earlier optimism. In *The Great Ascent,* he argued for a developmental view that saw success in identical terms for all peoples: the Western industrial paradigm would provide the pattern for the "lesser developed countries" of the Third World. This interpretation of success presumed an interpretation of human nature as universal and homogeneous, hence everywhere inspired by identical values. If one can see past all differences to some universal human condition, then one can enjoy the satisfaction of intellectual elegance. Whether optimistic or pessimistic, global judgments on man's fate or the human prospect all succumb to the

221

temptation toward intellectual certainty. The psychological appeal of despair is its lack of ambiguity. Even if the prospect is doom, at least, for once, one is sure.

This caution on the appeal of extreme positions — optimistic or pessimistic, Right or Left, utopian or dystopian — serves as a warning against misinterpretations of what we mean by a Voluntary History. We advertise no panacea, nor do we warn against inexorable collapse. The world we now inhabit is too complex, too ambiguous, too differentiated for any easy generalizations about great ascents or declines. This cautionary appeal strikes a note of skepticism regarding the more extreme claims on all three tactical fronts — the Left, the Right, and the Transformative — for we will probably experience in the decades ahead an ambiguous mixture of the values, virtues, and vices of all three. While each group hopes to convert the others from the errors of their ways, more than likely each of the groups will retain a solid core of unconverted advocates. So any ideological promise that requires universal conversion for its fulfillment is bound to be a promise that remains unfulfilled.

Our stance, then, is not to advocate some grand synthesis that would somehow sweep up all other alternatives into a solution free of conflicts. Rather we make an appeal to the advocates of various firm faiths: How are you going to live in a world where not everyone agrees with you? Can you accept something less than total victory, or must your adversaries choose among the options of conversion, annihilation, or repression?

For the Right and the Left, the problem of dissent has never been easy. Both right-wing and left-wing regimes have been known for ruthless and unpardonable suppressions of dissent; neither ideological extreme can claim innocence in this regard. While right-wing dictators and fascist regimes received more attention for acts of torture and repression, the Left mumbled apologies for Stalin as an aberration from the true principles of Marxist-Leninism. But recent years have produced a rash of defections from the ideological Left: from Alexsander Solzhenitsyn to "the New Philosophers" in France, who argue that the

Gulag and other Soviet atrocities are not historical accidents, but the inevitable outcome of a totalitarianism implicit in the tenets of the Marxist tradition. The Transformative Alternative tends to sidestep the issue of dissent altogether by assuming that its utopia is so attractive that no one could possibly dissent. Since universal transformation is the name of the game, even curmudgeons will come along when they see how beautiful it is. But neither conservatives nor radicals are noted for their susceptibility to ecstasy, so even the broadest based shift of paradigms will leave many behind. And what will be done with them? As with the Left and Right, so the Transformative Alternative will be plagued with dissent.

A Voluntary History requires the airing of differences that will abide. Nor is a glib affirmation of the freedom of speech sufficient to guarantee genuine diversity of views, for among the diverse groups will be some who take it unto themselves to deny others air time. Real pluralism is a subtle business, for among the plurality of interests will be some aspiring monists. In short, real freedom entails real conflicts. This point tends to go unnoticed by those on all three flanks who presume the supremacy of their own beliefs as a precondition for their success. The Right affirms as values both freedom and diversity, but then imagines that it can have law and order in the bargain. Once "the truth," which has been uttered by theoreticians from Edmund Burke to William Buckley, is seen, then, of course, everyone will agree that rugged individualism and the hidden hand will take care of all our problems. But not everyone will agree.

Those on the Left understand the sense in which *individualism* is itself a recent product of *social* history. Their vision of ideal social relationships defends collective interests by appealing to centralized planning implemented by an inevitable bureaucracy that is nonetheless responsive to the true needs of the people. In granting power to the people, the Left likewise presumes that everyone will agree on what these "true needs" are. Otherwise we would have to fall back on market mechanisms as a means of discerning what the people themselves want or need. This

223

presumption of true needs does not derive much support from the market already in place. On the contrary, the degree of diversification evident in the marketplace seems to contest the claim for any universal set of clearly specifiable true needs. Our truest and most human need — beyond the basics of animal survival — may be precisely the freedom to diversify. So the set of values defining the Left may be as inconsistent with the reality of diversity as is the Right's hope for utterly uncontested individual liberty. In both cases, the inevitability of real conflict is swept away by an assumption of universal agreement.

Devotees of the Transformative Alternative talk about The One as if it were already achieved. But if a transformational President were elected, he or she would still have to deal with the Defense Department, with real conflicts of interests among competing constituencies, with all of the old enmities listed in Chapter II (see page 18). Advocates of the Transformative Alternative see the tension of conflicting ideals through the lens of a paradigm for which disorder is a prelude to higher levels of order. They cite Nobel chemist Ilya Prigogine's theory of dissipative structures as an example of the way self-organizing systems generate coherence from seeming chaos. But advocates of systemic transformation often fail to note that in most cases (though not all) stress and disorder do not lead to higher forms but to decay and destruction.

Having placed a plague on all neatly constructed ideological houses, how do we propose to build a sustainable future? By some process of theoretical urban renewal — an urban removal that would sweep old structures from the landscape? On the contrary, ours is a process of renovation, a program for preserving the historical landmarks of our several traditions, for maintaining the rich human ecology of our differences. On specific issues we would look for a range of contributions from the Left, Right, and Transformative flanks. But in this concluding discussion we are addressing more a style of confrontation among the various flanks than a particular solution. We have no final solutions, no five-year plans. Instead, we agree with Don Michael (*On Learning to*

Plan—And Planning to Learn, 1973) that planning requires ongoing learning, not the forced imposition of some unrevisable future.

With respect to energy and the environment, for example, we can improve upon the adversarial deadlock that now poses business against environmentalists. The giant oil companies, the utilities, the nuclear power equipment manufacturers, the Nuclear Regulatory Commission, endless study commissions, and the Business Round Table all argue for the rapid development of all energy sources in the United States. They advocate strip mining, nuclear power, and new coal-burning plants. When they talk about the energy problem, they are talking about how to increase the supply of energy, not how to reduce demand.

Opposed to business interests, Friends of the Earth and the Sierra Club, SANE, the Clam Shell Alliance, the Abalone Alliance, and many others all stand against a set of technologies, especially nuclear power, whose nature they believe to be a rape of nature itself, foreclosing human options for a thousand generations to come. Endowed with such moral certainty, both sides claim righteousness on their side and demand total victory. Total victory means one side wins; the other side loses. The losing side no longer exists in the form it held before. It is repressed.

But tradeoffs are possible. When a corporation wishes to build a new plant and bring new jobs to a location already plagued by pollution, rather than forcing the company to conform to costly and nearly unattainable standards of near-zero pollution, a smaller investment could make a greater improvement in local air quality if spent on retrofitting older factories. In effect, a newcomer would buy a license to emit some amount of pollutants by reducing emissions from some existing plants by more than the new plant would add to the atmosphere. Because the cost of improvement is higher the closer one approaches perfection, improvements made on old plants will have more impact per dollar than designing further sophistication into relatively efficient new equipment. So the community as a whole can benefit from cleaner air, more jobs, and more productivity per dollar by

225

adopting a spirit of cooperation and inventiveness in tackling problems on an industry-wide basis rather than company by company.

This kind of cooperation requires a holistic grasp of environmental and economic issues combined with a knowledge of local conditions that cannot come from Washington. The statesmanship required for such tradeoffs demands the mediation of mutual interests, not regulations from on high. But if local groups remain deadlocked in sterile confrontations, then clumsier remedies will doubtless be imposed.

The MX missile system, for example, promises to be an extraordinarily clumsy attempt at providing national security. Here again a polarization between the Left and the Right pits equally unrealistic alternatives against one another. Neither massive spending on a mega-shell game nor unilateral disarmament will bring us closer to peaceful security. Nor can we assume that spiritual unity will allow us to transcend our differences with the Soviet Union. We do have enemies, and we are strong enough. We need not weaken our economy, and hence our real security, by draining limited capital and resources away from productive capacity into underground caverns. A narrow interest in high-tech weaponry leads military planners to ignore the social, economic, and psychological dimensions of security. An expanded vision of the real meaning of security could involve social and economic measures that would reduce our vulnerability to attack by decentralizing our concentrations of strategic resources. Nuclear power plants, for example, reduce our security by providing ideal targets for attack.

Freedom, finally, is our strongest weapon for maintaining national security — not the license of unrestricted individual liberty, but the freedom of different groups to place different normative constraints on the behavior of their members. Freedom does not mean that anything goes, nor is it a value that insists upon only one code of behavior. Instead, freedom allows *some* forms to flourish: not one, not all, but some.

By fostering a spirit of social experimentation, we satisfy an evolutionary principle of progress; Ashby's Law of Requisite Diversity states that in order to find the best solutions to evolutionary (or economic) problems of adaptation, a system needs to generate a variety of attempted solutions to be tested by trial and error. Though some attempts will fail, society as a whole will gain security from the successes of others.

Surely there would be inefficiencies if we tried everything. The whole point of maintaining a pluralistic stance toward the future is precisely to anticipate and avoid as many failures as possible. We will not attempt all futures; we need not settle on one; we will choose some. And by anticipating pitfalls we can turn what would be a ruthless social Darwinism — survival of the fittest — into a more benign social Lamarckism: an evolutionary process based on both diversity *and* purposive forethought.

The same logic of freedom through pluralism that guides economic evolution toward a successful and secure society also suggests a reconciliation between the Right's and Left's attitudes toward society's evolutionary failures. The welfare state assumes that it can take care of everybody. Right-wing rugged individualists preach every man for himself. A more sensible attitude toward welfare would admit that the range of personal responsibility can extend beyond the individual without reaching to all mankind. Each of us shares a responsibility, not for all, not for only one, but for some. We need a welfare system designed on the simple insight that the range of personal responsibility — like the capacity for devotion — can extend beyond the self without including the entire society.

Whether the topic is welfare, weaponry, or the economics of pollution, the American route toward a sustainable future will lead through freedom and diversity. Therefore it is essential that we understand the subtleties of pluralism. In complex systems, whether psyches or societies, total victory and repression cannot be attained. As ecologist and anthropologist Gregory Bateson often put it, the unit of survival is never the isolated individual or species, but always species-plus-environment. Pesticides and genocide are the errors of short-sighted absolutism that imagines it can eliminate evils without a self-destructive disruption of the human or biological ecosystem. According to an ecological ethic, rather than attempting to eliminate otherness, each group relates to other groups in a social structure of mutual interdependence.

Many of America's first settlers sought religious freedom. They allowed one another fervent devotions to different faiths. Though still very meaningful for many, religious orthodoxy no longer motivates the major life choices of most Americans. Nevertheless, the ideal of religious freedom serves as a model for handling our social and political faiths.

Because we have insisted on retaining a passionate commitment to *individual* freedom combined with unrestrained desires, we have created a paralyzed society adrift without vision in a turbulent and often dangerous world. If we continue on our present course, we will most likely encounter an increasingly authoritarian, war-ravaged future. If, instead, we recognize that freedom is more than the individual liberty to shrug off the needs of others, then we can learn to act cooperatively to take more control of our lives together. We can learn to give more and expect less. We can recognize that empathy, compassion, and security are inevitable handmaidens, and we can see through the fallacy of total victory in a diverse and pluralistic world. We may take heed from Alfred North Whitehead who once said, "It is the business of the future to be dangerous." It has always been dangerous, confronting as it does the unknown. For it is through the unknown that we transform our fears into knowledge and a richer understanding of what it means to be human.

Bibliography

Ackoff, Russell C. *Redesigning the Future: A Systems Approach to Societal Problems.* New York: John Wiley, 1974.

Anthony, William P. *Participative Management.* Reading, Massachusetts: Addison-Wesley, 1978.

Armstrong, J., and W. Harman. *Plausibility of a Restricted Energy Use Scenario.* Menlo Park, California: SRI International, 1975.

Aurobindo, Sri. *The Future Evolution of Man.* Pondecherry, India: Sri Aurobindo Ashram, 1963.

Barnet, Richard J. *The Lean Years: Politics in the Age of Scarcity.* New York: Simon and Schuster, 1980.

Barnet, Richard J., and Ronald E. Muller. *Global Reach: The Power of the Multinational Corporations.* New York: Simon and Schuster, 1975.

Barney, Gerald O., Study Director, *The Global 2000 Report to the President.* Washington, D.C.: Council on Environmental Quality and the Department of State, 1980.

Beer, Stafford. *Brain of the Firm: The Managerial Cybernetics of Organization.* London: Allen Lane, The Penguin Press, 1972.

Bell, Daniel. *The Coming of Post-Industrial Society: A Venture in Social Forecasting.* New York: Basic Books, 1973.

Beres, Louis Rene. *Apocalypse: Nuclear Catastrophe in World Politics.* Chicago: University of Chicago Press, 1980.

Bezold, Clement, ed. *Anticipatory Democracy: People in the Politics of the Future.* New York: Random House, Vintage Books, 1978.

"Blood in the Oil." *The Economist,* September 27, 1980.

Bowman, Jim et al. *The Far Side of the Future: Social Problems and Educational Reconstruction.* Washington, D.C.: World Future Society, 1978.

Braudel, Fernand. *The Mediterranean and the Mediterranean World in the Age of Philip II.* Vols. I and II, trans. Sian Reynolds. New York: Harper and Row, 1972 and 1974.

Brown, Lester R. *In the Human Interest: A Strategy to Stabilize World Population.* New York: W.W. Norton, 1974.

Brunner, John. *The Sheep Look Up.* New York: Ballantine Books, 1976.

Brzezinski, Zbigniew. *Between Two Ages: America's Role in the Technetronic Era.* New York: Viking Press, 1970.

Burns, Scott. *Home, Inc.* Garden City, New York: Doubleday & Company, Inc., 1975.

Bury, J.B. *The Idea of Progress.* New York: Macmillan, 1932.

Callenbach, Ernest. *Ecotopia: The Notebooks and Reports of William Weston.* New York: Bantam Books, 1977.

Carlson, Richard C., Sidney J. Everett, Willis W. Harman, Klaus W. Krause, Stephen Levy, Thomas F. Mandel, Paul C. Meagher, Lynn Rosener, Peter Schwartz, and Thomas C. Thomas. *California Energy Futures: Two Alternative Social Scenarios and Their Energy Implications.* Menlo Park, California: SRI International, 1980.

Commoner, Barry. *The Poverty of Power: Energy and Economic Crisis.* New York: Bantam Books, 1977.

Cornish, Edward, ed. *1999 The World of Tomorrow: Selections from The Futurist.* Washington, D.C.: World Future Society, 1978.

Curry, David, Richard Carlson, Clark Henderson, Thomas Mandel, Arnold Mitchell, Randall Pozdena, and Peter Schwartz. *Alternative Transportation Futures.* Menlo Park, California: Stanford Research Institute, 1976.

————. *Transportation in America's Future: Potentials for the Next Half Century.* Menlo Park, California: SRI International, 1977.

Daly, Herman E., ed. *Toward a Steady-State Economy.* San Francisco: W.H. Freeman and Company, 1973.

van Dam, J. "Energy in the Eighties — The Precarious Balance." A paper presented to the International Seminar for Academics in Hakone, Japan, September 1980.

Davis, Stanley M., and Paul R. Lawrence. *Matrix.* Reading, Massachusetts: Addison-Wesley, 1977.

Drucker, Peter F. *The Concept of the Corporation.* New York: New American Library, Mentor, 1964.

————. *The Age of Discontinuity.* New York: Harper and Row, 1968.

————. *Managing in Turbulent Times.* New York: Harper and Row, 1980.

Elgin, Duane. *City Size and the Quality of Life.* Menlo Park, California: SRI International, 1974.

————. "Limits to the Management of Large, Complex Systems," *An*

Assessment of Future National and International Problem Areas.
Vol. II. Menlo Park, California: SRI International, 1977.

————. *The Evolution of Consciousness and the Transformation
of Society.* Menlo Park, California: Stanford Research Institute,
1974.

Elgin, Duane, David C. MacMichael, and Peter Schwartz. *Alternative
Futures for Environmental Policy Planning: 1975-2000.* Menlo Park,
California: Stanford Research Institute, 1975.

Elgin, Duane, and Arnold Mitchell. "Voluntary Simplicity (2). *The Co-
Evolution Quarterly,* Summer, 1977.

Emery, F.E., and E.L. Trist. *Towards a Social Ecology: Contextual
Appreciation of the Future in the Present.* London: Plenum Press,
1973.

Enzensberger, Hans Magnus. *The Consciousness Industry: On Litera-
ture, Politics and the Media.* New York: Seabury Press, Continuum,
1974.

Falk, Richard A. *A Study of Future Worlds.* New York: Free Press,
1975.

Gabor, D. *The Mature Society.* New York: Praeger Publishers, 1972.

Gershuny, Jonathan. *After Industrial Society? The Emerging Self-
Service Economy.* London: The MacMillan Press Ltd., 1978.

Ghelardi, Robert. *Economics, Society and Culture.* New York: Dell
Publishing, 1976.

Gregg, R. "Voluntary Simplicity," 19361. Reprinted in *Manas,* September 4 & 11, 1974.

Gribbin, John. *Forecasts, Famines and Freezes.* New York: Walker and
Co., 1976.

Gross, Bertram. "Friendly Fascism." *Social Policy,* November/Decem-
ber, 1970.

Hackett, John W., Sir. *The Third World War.* New York: Macmillan
Publishing Co., Inc., 1979.

Harman, Willis W. *An Incomplete Guide to the Future.* San Francisco:
San Francisco Book Company, 1976.

————. "The Potential Use and Misuse of Consciousness Technologies," *An Assessment of Future National and International Problem
Areas.* Vol. II. Menlo Park, California: SRI International, 1977.

Heilbroner, R. *An Inquiry into the Human Prospect.* New York: W.W.
Norton, 1974.

————. *Business Civilization in Decline.* New York: W.W. Norton,
1976.

Heiliger, Wilhelm S. *Soviet and Chinese Personalities.* Lanham, Mary-
land: University Press of America, Inc., 1980.

Henderson, Hazel. *Creating Alternative Futures: The End of Economics*. New York: Berkley, Windhover, 1978.

Hirsch, Fred. *Social Limits to Growth*. Cambridge, Massachusetts: Harvard University Press, 1977.

Howard, Ted, and Jeremy Rifkin. *Who Should Play God? The Artificial Creation of Life and What It Means for the Future of the Human Race*. New York: Dell, 1977.

Illich, Ivan. *Tools for Conviviality*. New York: Harper and Row, 1973.

————. *Toward a History of Needs*. New York: Pantheon Books, 1977.

Jantsch, Erich, and Conrad Waddington, eds. *Evolution and Consciousness: Human Systems in Transition*. Reading, Massachusetts: Addison-Wesley, 1976.

Johnson, Warren. *Muddling Toward Frugality*. Boulder, Colorado: Shambhala Publications, 1978.

Jouvenel, Bertrand De. *The Art of Conjecture*. Trans. Nikita Lary. New York: Basic Books, 1967.

————. *On Power: Its Nature and the History of Its Growth*. Trans. J.F. Huntington. Boston: Beacon Press, 1962

Kahn, Herman, ed. *The Future of the Corporation*. New York: Mason & Lipscomb, 1974.

Kahn, Herman et al. *The Next Two Hundred Years*. New York: William Morrow & Co., Inc., 1976.

Laqueur, Walter. *Terrorism*. Boston: Little, Brown and Company, 1977.

Laszlo, Ervin et al. *Goals for Mankind: A Report to the Club of Rome on the New Horizons of Global Community*. New York: E.P. Dutton, 1977.

Leiss, William. *The Limits to Satisfaction: On Needs and Commodities*. London: Marion Boyars, 1978.

Lekachman, Robert. "The Crash of 1980." *The Nation*, July 5, 1980, pp. 14-18.

Mandel, Thomas F., Barbara De Caro, William Lee, Floyd Lewis, Roger Mack, Randall Pozdena, and Peter Schwartz. *Transportation Energy Demand in Alternative Futures*. Menlo Park, California: SRI International, 1978.

Mark, Jerome A. "Productivity Developments." *Looking Ahead and Projection Highlights,* Volume IV, Number 4.

Markley, O.W. "Human Consciousness in 'Transformation,'" in E. Jontsch & C. Waddington, eds. *Evolution and Consciousness: Human Systems in Transition*. Reading, Massachusetts: Addison-Wesley, 1976.

Markley, O.W., Joseph Campbell, Duane Elgin, Willis Harman, Arthur Hastings, Floyd Mason, Brendan O'Regan, and Leslie Schneider. *Changing Images of Man*. Menlo Park, California: Stanford Research Institute, 1974.

_____. *Contemporary Societal Problems*. Menlo Park, California: SRI International, 1971.

Maruyama, Magoroh, and Arthur Harkins, eds. *Cultures Beyond the Earth*. New York: Random House, Vintage Books, 1975.

_____. *Cultures of the Future*. The Hague: Mouton Publishers, 1978.

McEachron, Norman B., and Peter J. Teige. "Constraints on Large-Scale Technological Projects," *An Assessment of Future National and International Problem Areas*. Vol. II. Menlo Park, California: SRI International, 1977.

McHale, John. *The Future of the Future*. New York: George Braziller, 1969.

McHale, John, and Magda Cordell McHale. *Futures Studies: An International Survey*. New York: United Nations Institute for Training and Research, 1975.

Meadows, Donella H. et al. *The Limits to Growth*. New York: Universe Books, 1974.

Mesarovic, Mihajlo, and Eduard Pestel. *Mankind at the Turning Point: The Second Report to the Club of Rome*. New York: E.P. Dutton, 1974.

Michael, Donald N. *The Unprepared Society*. New York: Harper and Row Publishers, Inc., 1970.

Michael, Donald N. *On Learning to Plan and Planning to Learn*. San Francisco: Jossey-Bass Publishers, 1973.

Mitchell, Arnold. *Lifeways and Lifestyles*. Menlo Park, California: Stanford Research Institute, 1973.

_____. "Changing Values and Lifestyles." Speech based on VALS Report No. 1. Menlo Park, California: SRI International, 1979.

_____. "The Effects of Stress on Individuals and Society," *An Assessment of Future National and International Problem Areas*. Vol. II. Menlo Park, California: SRI International, 1977.

Moffitt, Michael. "The Third World: Deeper in Debt." *The Nation*, July 5, 1980, pp. 18-20.

Ogilvy, James. *Many Dimensional Man*. New York: Oxford University Press, 1977; New York: Harper Colophon, 1979.

Pirages, D.C., and Ehrlich, P.R. *Ark Two: Social Response to Environmental Imperatives*. San Francisco: W.H. Freeman and Co., 1974.

Pye, Lucian W., ed. *Communications and Political Development*. Princeton, New Jersey: Princeton University Press, 1963.

233

Reuyl, John S. et al. *Solar Energy in America's Future: A Preliminary Assessment*. Menlo Park, California: SRI International, 1977.

Rhyne, Russell F. *Projecting Whole-Body Future Patterns — The Field Anomaly Relaxation (Far) Method*. Menlo Park, California: SRI International, 1971.

Richardson, J. David. "Current World Trends." *New International Realities*, October 1979.

Rockefeller Brothers Fund. *The Unfinished Agenda: Policy Guide to Environmental Issues*. New York: T.Y. Crowell Co., 1977.

Royal Ministry for Foreign Affairs in Cooperation with the Secretariat for Future Studies. *To Choose a Future: A Basis for Discussion and Deliberations on Future Studies in Sweden*, trans. Rudy Feichtner. Stockholm: Swedish Institute, 1974.

Sanders, Lawrence. *The Tommorrow File*. New York: Berkley Medallion Books, 1976.

Schneider, Steven H., and Lynne E. Mesirow. *The Genesis Strategy: Climate and Global Survival*. New York: Plenum Press, 1976.

Schumacher, E.F. *Small Is Beautiful: Economics As If People Mattered*. New York: Harper and Row, Perennial Library, 1973.

Schwartz, Peter, Willis W. Harman, Harold A. Linstone, Duane Elgin, Pamela Kruzic, O.W. Markley, Norman McEachron, Arnold Mitchell, Benjamin Suta, and Peter J. Teige. *An Assessment of Future National and International Problem Areas*. Vol. I. Menlo Park, California: SRI International, 1977.

————. "The Growing Conflict Between Central Control and Individual Freedom," *An Assessment of Future National and International Problem Areas*. Vol. II. Menlo Park, California: SRI International, 1977.

Singer, Benjamin D. *Feedback and Society: A Study of the Uses of Mass Channels for Coping*. Lexington, Massachusetts: D.C. Heath, Lexington Books, 1973.

Sites, Joseph L., Col., John F. Scott et al. *Futures Group Periodic Report-3*. Carlisle Barracks, Pennsylvania: Strategic Studies Institute, U.S. Army War College, November 1980.

Taber, Robert. *The War of the Flea*. New York: Citadel Press, 1970.

Tannenbaum, Arnold S. et al. *Hierarchy in Organizations*. San Francisco: Jossey-Bass Publishers, 1974.

Thurow, Lester C. *The Zero-Sum Society*. New York: Basic Books, 1980.

Toffler, Alvin. *The Third Wave*. New York: William Morrow and Co., Inc., 1980.

————. *Future Shock*. New York: Bantam Books, 1971.

————. *The Ecospasm Report*. New York: Bantam Books, 1975.

Valery, Paul. *The Collected Works of Paul Valery: History and Politics*. Vol. 10. Trans. Denise Folliot and Jackson Mathews. Princeton, New Jersey: Princeton University Press, Bollingen Series, 1962.

Weber, Max. *The Protestant Ethic and the Spirit of Capitalism*. Trans. Talcott Parsons. New York: Charles Scribner's Sons, 1958.